The End of our Exploring

Also by Monica Furlong

WITH LOVE TO THE CHURCH

TRAVELLING IN

CONTEMPLATING NOW

The End of our Exploring

by

MONICA FURLONG

HODDER AND STOUGHTON
LONDON SYDNEY AUCKLAND TORONTO

... the end of all our exploring
Will be to arrive where we started
And know the place for the first time.

T. S. ELIOT, *Little Gidding*

In memory of Alfred Furlong,
1889-1972.

Acknowledgments

Quotations from the songs of George Harrison are reprinted with his permission and that of Harrisongs Ltd.

'Let It Bleed' is quoted by permission of the Rolling Stones.

'All You Need Is Love', words and music by John Lennon and Paul McCartney, is quoted by permission of Northern Songs Ltd. © 1967.

'The Minister' by R. S. Thomas is quoted from *Song at the Year's Turning* by permission of Rupert Hart-Davis Ltd.

Stevie Smith's poem is quoted from *Selected Poems* by permission of the Longman Group Ltd.

My especial thanks are due to Mrs. Joan Horton for typing the manuscript.

Contents

Part I

In Search of Meaning

WE LIVE IN A PERIOD IN WHICH IT IS NOT POSSIBLE to talk meaningfully about God. People still try to do so, of course, but they gradually become aware of difficulties which would not have troubled our ancestors. They find they must do it with a wryness and humour which is a kind of apology for slipping into a vocabulary that is not truly acceptable. Or they find they must do it with an excessive fervour which somehow embarrasses and alienates those with whom they are trying to hold a conversation. Or they find that they are searching for words and ideas outside the traditional field of theology in an attempt to make what they say meaningful for themselves and others, so that, for example, Christ becomes the archetypal hero, and God the 'ground of our being'.

The problem is not, it should be noted, that we have ceased to want to talk about numinous experiences. The groping to do so goes on and there seems no good reason that it should cease so long as there are men left on earth. We need to know if there is meaning in the Universe to know what sort of creatures we are ourselves. We *may* need (though this seems to me rather more doubtful and many humanists would not agree) some knowledge about the kind of world it is to have any sort of coherent moral system. What does seem clear is that these are questions that we cannot leave permanently unanswered either in our private or our collective lives. We cannot live without *any* sense of meaning; the meaning may be a limited one like our love for one person, or supporting a family, or trying to succeed at a job, but without some such meaning in our life we cannot carry on. And then there is often a kind of compulsion in us to search for some deeper foundation upholding our private structure of meaning; to relate our love for one person to a general theory about the meaning of love in the world, for instance, or to look at our efforts to keep one family going in the context of the way our whole society organises itself into familiar groups. We seem to have a tendency to look for meaning, however limited, and when we are deprived of it, to feel suicidal. A prisoner in Auschwitz has described how, when he and a number of fellow-prisoners were put to work repairing and demolishing bombed buildings in the camp, they managed to keep going, despite starvation rations, long hours, and extreme brutality. When, however, this task was completed, and they were set to carry heavy weights of sand from one end of the compound to the other, only to have to carry them back again the next day, then despair set in, and men who had survived near-intolerable hardships, suddenly gave up, and threw themselves on the electric wire, or lay down and let the guards kick them to death. The very limited meaning left in their lives had been taken from them.

Just as we cannot leave the question of meaning unanswered in the general shape and direction of our lives, so we cannot leave it unanswered where moral questions are concerned. 'The problems of conduct,' says R. M. Hare in *The Language of Morals,* 'though sometimes less diverting than crossword puzzles, have to be solved in a way that crossword puzzles do not. We cannot wait to see the solution in the next issue, because on the solution of the problems depends what happens in the next issue.'

Many religious people of traditional mould would feel that we have put ourselves in a position where we cannot hope to answer either the problem of meaning or the problem of conduct because we have somehow lost, or destroyed, our faith. They see the decline in church-going, the loss of interest in the language of the churches, and the radical change in moral customs, particularly sexual customs, as a huge loss of sense of meaning, and because they have been trained, more particularly by an acquaintance with the Old Testament, to think of God in very personal terms, they talk about this change in the language of defection and betrayal.

It does seem as if there is a loss of a sense of meaning, a loss to which the high suicide figures seem to contribute evidence, though one might point to sociological facts, as well as religious

ones, which have helped to bring about the present situation —
the growth of conurbations together with the disappearance of
smaller communities, the collapse of the extended family, the
increased mobility of the population, and the disintegrative effect
of two gigantic wars in the first half of the century. Under such
stresses people become aware that they are less meaningful for
others, and lacking this affirmation feel less meaningful to themselves. It may be that this loss has made us all less capable of
maintaining traditional attitudes to religion, or it may be that the
loss of traditional attitudes has made us less able to maintain
social cohesion. Whatever the origin of the situation, it does
appear that we have partially lost something that was precious
to our sense of well-being.

It is recoverable, and if so, in what form? The traditional
religious bodies of this country still talk at times as if we might
recover the sense of meaning in its old form. They sound as if
they believe that, given a reformed Church, and a better trained
and deployed clergy and laity, the people of this country might
be persuaded to flock to the churches, and that this action on
their part would be accompanied by changes of heart and mind
which would not only solve the problem of meaning, but would
relieve, if not remove, many of the painful social problems with
which we are beset.

Is this really a likely thing to happen, and if likely, is it desir-
able? In this generation we have seen not merely a considerable
decline in church-going but a sharp decline in the numbers of
those offering themselves for ordination, and bringing forward
children for baptism and confirmation. Incurable optimists will,
of course, insist that the setback is only temporary, and that this
swing of the pendulum will be succeeded by a swing in the
Church's favour towards the end of the century. More realistic
Christians see the Church's function as changing to that of a
minority group, exerting a minority influence, rather perhaps as
the Quakers have done in English history.

But if the ambition of the optimists were achieved would it
necessarily be a good thing? The parochial structure of the Church
of England, and the congregational structure of the Roman
Catholic and the Free Churches, are now only faintly relevant
to the way in which we live; in general it is only in village life that
what takes place in the church is any kind of expression of the

daily life of the congregation, and so of the kind of love-hate relationship with one's fellow-man to which the act of receiving Communion with him might seem significant. Nor does the sort of episodic pattern of Church observance seem any more relevant. Neither the feast days of saints, nor the lives of most of the saints themselves feel important to most of us, and we may feel that there are many more creative ways of spending our Sunday than spending a precious hour of it in an old building among strangers.

These considerations are of little importance, however, compared to a much bigger question which is whether the Church is still an adequate vessel for the kind of meaning we are seeking. One of the difficulties is the age of the Church. Rooted as she is in history, she carries the limitations of this as much as any other institution. Thus, certain political attitudes (however vigorously denied by present members of the Church) and certain moral attitudes, established over centuries, make it difficult for her members to see beyond a particular framework and imagine what life could be like without it. But this is an age not of faith, but of cathartic doubt, and unless everything can, potentially at least, be questioned, then there is a kind of betrayal of the spirit of the times. It seems possible that doubt *is* our search for meaning, and that whatever refuses this painful path has cut itself off from our search for life.

Another of the important developments of our time lies in our new awareness of ourselves as members, not of nations, but of the race of mankind. In the jargon phrase the world has become a 'global village'. Again the history of the Church betrays her. Associated as she has been with Western societies, and particularly with empire-building societies, with their inevitable superiority over the conquered, and so over their beliefs and ideas, she has no habit, no life-style, of being able to listen to spiritual truths which are not her own. But no such superiority will be possible in the future. Hungry for meaning as we are, and exposed to new sources of spirituality, we shall turn in whatever direction we are likely to be fed; Buddhism or Hinduism, Judaism or Islam, Zen Buddhism or agnosticism, we are too hungry to care.

What seems likely is that instead of being *the* source in the West of spiritual enlightenment, the Church will become one of a number of sources, only some of which will seek any kind of formal organisation at all. There is a sense in which the growth of formal organisation indicates the breakdown of religious experience. While men are enjoying dynamic experiences in their daily lives, as for instance the Apostles at the time of Pentecost, then formality is not necessary. But as the ecstatic experiences die away then comes the need to establish a framework which tries to give permanence to particular insights, and in which it is hoped profound religious experiences will from time to time recur. There is thus built up a body of experience about men's spiritual adventures, which both enables them to recur but also acts as a brake upon their recurring too often. (Too often being when they pose too much of a threat to men's sanity or the continuity of their lives.)

It seems possible that in the future no formal religion will be treated as seriously as in the past but rather that men will feel freer to search for what they need among a number of traditions, in the end not feeling the need to ally themselves wholly with any one of them. Such apprenticeship and discipline as they require may be very different from the sort deemed necessary in the past, and the gurus to which they turn may be unrecognisable as such by past and present standards.

One of the advantages of such a revolution will be that it recognises that all men are engaged upon a spiritual search and not only those, as various religious confessions tend to suggest, who are occupied with particular forms of belief.

Spiritually-minded people oppose the life of the man who works inwardly for his liberation to the life of the average man who, according to them, does not do any inner work of this nature. This opposition is erroneous. The only real difference between these two men is that the first makes his intention to achieve total realisation explicit, while the second does not make it explicit. But all men work, whether they know it or not, to overcome their fundamental lack, to resolve the problem of their unsatisfactory condition. . . . All that man does is aimed at compensating a fundamental disharmony.[1]

All men, in other words, are striving for wholeness. If formal religion, and the concept of God, help them in this then they will

[1] Hubert Benoit, *Let Go* (Allen & Unwin, 1962).

use them gladly, but if not they will abandon them without (unless made to feel guilty by others) feelings of defection.

An interesting modern commentator about man's struggle for wholeness was C. G. Jung, who compared what has happened to Christianity to an earlier phase of history. 'The gods of Hellas and Rome perished from the same disease as did our Christian symbols; men discovered then, as they do today, that they had no thoughts whatever on the subject.'[2] Jung knew of the importance for man of finding life religiously meaningful, but did not believe that Christianity was a kind of glove-puppet which might be brought to life by inserting an eager hand. Instead he suggested a path which was a kind of abstraction of centuries of religious and psychological insights which he called individuation. Individuation did not call upon a man to undertake the discipline of any particular religious body, nor was it the same for each person. As its name implied it was a path peculiar to the person who undertook it, imposing upon him his own particular discipline, possibly of a very extreme kind. Jung did not believe that this path was for everyone; the majority, in his view, were not ready to depart from conformity and convention. But a few were, and are, striking out towards a goal, the goal of wholeness. When they succeeded, even partially, he believed that they brought a healing awareness not only to themselves, but to the world around them. At times he uses language reminiscent of an older view of man's journey. 'Salvation does not come from going along or from running away. Nor does it come from letting oneself be carried along without willing. Salvation comes from complete self-surrender, and one's gaze must be directed upon a centre.'[3]

Jung had borrowed substantially from far older attempts to describe man's journey — from literature, from the folk-legend which underlies it, and from the myths which are at the heart of all men's attempts at story-telling. To Jung, as to a modern anthropologist, a myth was not an idle, fanciful tale, but a profound dissection of the ancestral experience of life in this world with its varied diet of joy and suffering, of peace and terror, of awe and banality. Myth is the core of life itself as man has known it; in his need to discover an order in which he can live, he has

² C. G. Jung, *The Integration of the Personality* (Routledge & Kegan Paul, 1940).
³ Ibid.

compulsively talked and written about his experience. But it is not just that he has made up a story about it. Myth is more dynamic than that. It is not so much that man has experiences and then writes stories, as that the stories — the same stories with certain variations — have a way of living themselves out in human society even in widely spaced cultures and civilizations. Oedipus, Odysseus, Lancelot and Guinevere, Faust, are (to those who hold this view of myth) not just people in books, but are in a sense part of the fabric of our own lives and the lives of those we know.

The myths, and the literature which has been spun from them, seem to have an obsession with the theme of quest or journey. It is a kind of *leit-motiv* throughout human culture. Thus from primitive folk-tales to the high art of *The Odyssey*, from renewal rites and fertility cults to the poems of St. John of the Cross, from the advice of doctors and the pastoral teachings of priests to Jung's elaborate theory of individuation, men have been strug-gling to express something deeply felt about the human condition. It is that it is not a senseless jumble of events, but rather some-thing with a beginning, a middle and an end. That it is a process which has meaning, and in which progress is possible. Man begins in one place and ends in another, having done some strenuous travelling in between. (Or, more subtly, he returns to the place he started from, but sees it with new eyes.)

There is, I suggest, no theme (not even love itself) which has shown itself more dominant in the world's literature than the theme of the journey. Wherever we look in folk-tale, art, religious teaching, we find evidence, however fragmentary, of a hero setting out from a haven which has become constricting, undergoing a series of adventures which have a transforming effect, and eventually reaching, or failing to reach, his goal, or prize, or spiritual home.

It would be foolish to ignore that there has been one stream within our Western culture that has talked explicitly of journey where the myths and fables talked only implicitly — the stream of Christianity. Within its generous intellectual and cultural traditions there have been a number of approaches to the idea of journey, some seeing it in terms of the salvation of the individual soul, some in terms of the salvation of all humankind, some (the mystics) being more concerned with moving into relationship with God, in particular the wholeness of *unio mystica*. In the West it has been the most continuous and courageous of the struggles to seek meaning in the puzzling and often contradictory lot of man.

In our own time men find it difficult to listen to talk of journey from that particular source, though they try, often in ways that strike onlookers as dangerous or bizarre, to find a journey for themselves. The return to primitive forms of journey such as witchcraft and astrology; the new found interest in meditation and in contemplative forms of experience; the adoption of Eastern forms of religion, particularly Buddhism, Zen Buddhism, and Vedantism; the attempt to understand something new about the meaning of the group, by group dynamics, and new forms of communal living; the turning to drugs, especially LSD and cannabis, in an attempt to learn something new about the self and its meaning; the expression and sharing of some of this ferment of thought in pop music and musicals like *Hair*; all these seem to me to be attempts to set out upon, or talk about, an inner journey. Perhaps the contemporary experience, however fragmentary our understanding of it, can give us some idea of the shape of our present longing.

What needs to be worked out is whether there is a journey for us now, and if so, what form it can possibly take. To write of journey at all implies that man believes his life has meaning, and contains a hope of fulfilment. Not that fulfilment is necessarily quite what we expect, in fact it may be that it is never the fulfilment the hero hoped for or foresaw at the beginning of his journey. The journey is essentially a learning process, often of an acutely painful and humiliating kind, so that bit by bit the hero becomes a changed man whose needs and satisfactions may be very different from those of the callow youth who set out. His eventual triumph may express itself, as with Odysseus, in the joy of homecoming, or it may depend, as with Job, upon having his eyes opened upon a world of awe and majesty and beauty that robs him of all argument with his fate. But even the most tragic myths such as that of Gilgamesh, do not see man's life as meaningless. The 'bare, fork'd animal' may be shovelled like rubbish into a mass-grave at Auschwitz, or endure the slower mortification of old age and disease, but the burning life that flickers in and through him has a way of reflecting meaning, even in, perhaps particularly in, situations of the most extreme suffering and despair.

What the journeys are describing is religious experience, not using 'religion' in any ecclesiastical or doctrinal sense, but in the sense of its earlier meaning i.e. *relegere* — to gather together. The stories of journey are a gathering together of innumerable scraps of experience and wisdom, and the literary form that they take embraces the hope that together they add up to a meaning of crucial importance to every one of us. They are the pieces of a jigsaw of which the authors have only a few fragments. The *opus* — of completing the design — goes on, and we are invited to take our own part in producing pieces and fitting them in.

It is tempting to feel that we ourselves are somehow untouched by the myths and exempted from the laborious and humbling duty to 'gather together'. We sense danger in the realm of 'meaning', in particular the danger of self-awareness, and we may try to escape by ignoring the living presence of the myths as they touch our lives. Yet to choose meaninglessness may make our lives so wretched that we will be forced to narcotise ourselves as many already do, or to inject a spurious meaning into a limited objective like social reform or obtaining political power; or, of course, to drift towards more violent methods of filling our emptiness, such as war.

Meaning is difficult and painful for us to discuss — we find it much more embarrassing than the Victorians found sex — yet it has a way of forcing itself upon our attention and (again like sex) shaping our lives whether we want it to or not. But we seem to have no vocabulary with which to discuss it, because it seems unlikely that we can continue to hope to discuss our problem adequately within the framework of traditional Christianity. Its language is now so worn that it can be, and is, used as a way of stopping thought and preventing experience, and it is this which lends so much of Christian discussion a parochial air that makes it irrelevant to man and his journeys. Again there are signs that organised Christianity is unaware, or perhaps afraid of, the treasure that lies at its heart, and it might be that others may find it and live in the light of it before the guardians of the treasure see what it is they guard. Maybe this is the way the harlots go first into the kingdom of God.

In this book I have tried to look at several sorts of journey which seem relevant to our struggle for meaning. The first of these is Jung's journey of individuation, as he called it, a psychoanalytic attempt to describe what 'salvation' could mean. The second sort of journey, often overlapping with Jung's theory of individuation, is that revealed in well-known folk-tales and fables. These illuminate what it *used* to mean to be the hero or journeying man, and I have included them because the crises described so often seem to be similar to the crises which afflict us. The third sort of journey is the one outlined by Christianity. Whether or not we still feel Christianity is part of our journey it has shaped our culture and our common assumptions and we are deeply influenced by it when we try to think about meaning. The fourth sort of journey is a much more scrappy and tentative affair, since I have tried to talk about what has happened over the last few years and is happening now, and obviously later perspectives will make nonsense of some of this.

Finally, I have tried to take something from each of other journeys, to see which parts of them we might try to make our own in the future, and which parts we must reject as impeding our progress. It will become apparent, I hope, that I do believe in a journey, though the flickering fitful light of meaning makes it a frustrating, and faintly absurd, task to try to describe it. The journey itself has a way of making nonsense of whatever we try to say, in fact, we shall only know that we ourselves are engaged upon the journey when we find language breaking beneath our feet as experience destroys the formulas and dogmas like so many idols. There is terror as well as joy in such a discovery, the discovery that life brims with meaning, and that the journey itself matters in ways that we can only dimly grasp.

CHAPTER TWO

Journey of Individuation

ALMOST ALONE AMONG WESTERN THINKERS JUNG SETS
out a modern version of the journey, a road to salvation
which the twentieth-century pilgrim can choose to travel. Or
rather perhaps, a road by which he can let himself be chosen.
Nobody is likely to set off on the path of individuation, as Jung
calls it, lightly, or perhaps even if they feel any other course is
really open to them. It is a vocation, a drive in man or woman
which makes itself felt in dreams, fantasies, moods and actions.
If you do not have the vocation, or if you try to imitate another
man's method instead of discovering the 'way' within yourself,
then no amount of effort will help. As the Chinese proverb says
'If the wrong man uses the right means, the right means works
in the wrong way.'

This sounds so much like the Christian idea that 'many are
called but few are chosen' or Christ's teaching that 'strait is the
gate and narrow is the way that leads to life' that it is tempting
to begin to think (at least for those who have been conditioned
by Christian thinking) that Jung is merely finding new ways of
expressing older ideas of salvation. But it is as naive to suppose
this as to take the over-defensive stance of some Christians. Jung
uses many insights which have been crucial in Christianity, but
he also makes abundant use of ideas (Gnosticism and alchemy
in particular) which the Church has traditionally regarded either
as heretical or at the very least misguided. He is also deeply influenced by Eastern thought and by Buddhist thought in particular. And through all his thinking and writing two other very
profound influences are at work. One is his vast knowledge of
primitive mythology, the other is his deep knowledge of the

human mind, in sickness and in health, as he was daily confronted with its conscious and unconscious manifestations in the course of his work.

Instead of beginning from a religious theory and trying to fit human experience into it (discovering in the process that some bits fit magnificently and others don't fit at all), Jung has tried to begin at the end of human experience. Instead of drawing a map of God, in the way that dogma tends to do, he has tried to draw the shape of the hole he finds in man, and then to see which of man's attempts to fill this hole have been most successful, a task which he sets about with a singular lack of prejudice.

He does, of course, have a cosmology, but Jung's cosmology is set within man himself, and it is there that he proposes that we shall find, or not find, God. Jung sees man's history as a long struggle to free himself from the state of unconsciousness. Primitive man was not aware of himself as 'I'. He was immersed in the tribe with its codes and rituals, and perhaps even more totally he was immersed in the natural life around him. His own fears and joys blended inextricably with his environment, in a way which we can still perceive in young children. A rock, a tree, a whirlpool becomes a devil, an incarnation of terror. Triumphs in hunting, the fertility of crops, and of tribal communities, food, warmth, well-being, health, are the blessing of benevolent gods.

As man becomes more conscious, as he develops an 'ego', he not only differentiates himself from the tribe, coming to see that his own best interests are not necessarily totally identified with theirs, but he also withdraws many of his projections from the world around him. The rock and the tree become just a rock and a tree; he can separate them from his inner fears even when these are considerable. As the devils become fewer so the gods become fewer. The gods, or God, are no longer wedded just to material needs, but are part of a more amorphous longing, the need to grow inwardly, or change, or become something that one was not to start with.

The 'ego' which man has developed with so much pain and effort makes it possible for him to take a certain realistic grasp on the world around him. It is the opposite of the state of 'possession'. It lends a certain continuity to all the innumerable states of thought and feeling which go to make up a man's daily experience; all can be referred back to an 'I' which takes them to itself. But if the ego is the flower on the tree, the roots of the tree plunge down, out of sight, into the rich soil of the unconscious. The unconscious contributes every moment of the time to the conscious personality. Our every word, gesture, expression, mood, fantasy, dream, is nourished by this unseen life. 'The unconscious', says Jung, 'is the mother of consciousness.'[1]

Nor, in Jung's view, is it only our own unconscious from which we draw. On a deeper level we are in touch with the 'collective unconscious', the primitive myths and images which have occupied man in every culture and in every period. Just as every man's body is a museum of man's biological development, containing within it vestiges of innumerable evolutionary stages, so man's mind carries within it the whole history of the unconscious giving birth to consciousness. 'The conscious mind is based upon, and results from, an unconscious psyche, which is prior to consciousness and continues to function together with, or despite, consciousness.'[2]

Well-being, either for the individual or for society, consists of giving full value to both ego and unconscious. If the ego is swamped in the uprush of unconscious material, then the individual suffers from what we know as madness. If a community is similarly overwhelmed, then we witness a collective madness which may take the form of war, genocide, or a 'reign of terror'. If, on the other hand, man tries to pretend that he is his 'ego', that there is nothing to him apart from what he is conscious of, then he inflicts a different sort of damage upon himself. He is cutting himself off from his roots, the roots of instinct, intuition, myth and numinous experience. He cannot behave in such a way without posing a grave threat to his sexuality, to his ability to relate to others, and finally, and most seriously, to his ability to find life meaningful. His attempt to apply rationality in areas of his life where it is not appropriate interferes with his capacity to feel and expresses itself in neurosis. Increasingly he becomes afraid of his inner world, since the more it is denied the more threatening it becomes, and his life becomes a headlong flight from it, a flight assisted by all the apparatus of a world similarly bent on denying its own nature.

[1] *The Integration of the Personality*, pp. 12, 13.
[2] Ibid.

The enormous increase of technical facilities only serves to occupy the mind with all sorts of sensations and impressions that lure the attention and interest from the inner world. The relentless flood of newspapers, radio programmes and movies may widen or fill the external mind, while at the same time, and in the same measure, consciousness of the inner world becomes darkened and may eventually disappear altogether. But 'forgetting' is not identical with 'getting rid of'. On the contrary, the situation has become worse: instead of facing the enemy, we risk being attacked from the rear, where we are unaware and defenceless.[3]

Once it is denied, the unconscious becomes extremely dangerous to us. 'If an individual deviates too much from the original instinctive pattern', says Jung, 'then he realizes the full impact of the unconscious forces.'[4] As with the individual, so with the community. When we reject the patient, often humiliating, effort to live in tune with the unconscious, what we expose ourselves to is the risk of possession, possession which may take place with very little awareness on our part until we find ourselves caught up in forms of destruction inimical to all that consciousness has painfully achieved. 'Rationalism and doctrinairism', says Jung, 'are the diseases of our time . . . nowadays most people identify themselves almost exclusively with their consciousness, and imagine that they are only what they know about themselves.'[5] This overvaluing of reason leads to a pauperisation of the individual.

Man can no longer create fables. As a result, a great deal escapes him; for it is important and salutary to speak also of incomprehensible things.[6] Nowadays we can see as never before that the peril which threatens all of us comes not from nature, but from man, from the psyches of the individual and the mass. The psychic aberration of man is the danger. Everything depends upon whether or not our psyche functions properly. If certain persons lose their heads nowadays, a hydrogen bomb will go off.[7]

[3] Ibid., p. 10.   [4] Ibid., p. 14.
[5] C. G. Jung, *Memories, Dreams, Reflections* (Fontana, 1967) p. 330.
[6] Ibid., p. 331.   [7] Ibid., p. 154.

We have then a situation in which man has cut himself off from his roots, and is enduring the neurosis and despair which this inflicts upon him. He is deprived alike of his instincts, his faith, and the myths which spoke to him of journey. What, if any, is the answer in such a predicament?

Part of the answer undoubtedly lies in individuals discovering that they cannot live in such a way. The more desperately they seek to control their lives by rationality alone the more they become subjects of irrationality. Depression, insomnia, stress diseases, various forms of addiction come more and more to dominate their lives. Loneliness, a form of grief which no amount of reason can comfort, eats into their souls. Goaded by such symptoms and others, many begin, with or without the help of psychotherapy, to ask questions about their own psyche and to question the values of the society which despises the riches of the unconscious. Gradually they learn not to be afraid of the disturbing feelings within, to befriend them, and listen to them, and let them have their proper place in their lives.

There is, however, in Jung's view, a personal development that goes beyond this one, and this is described in his theory of individuation. The goal of individuation is wholeness. 'By it', says Jung, 'I mean the psychological process that makes of a human being an "individual" — a unique, indivisible unit or "whole man".'[8] Most of us are very far from being 'whole men' because of our inability or failure to integrate parts of our unconscious which are crucial to the realisation of the self. Because of our fear of the unconscious we place too much emphasis on the ego. But the man who has embarked on the process of individuation knows that the ego is merely the 'centre of consciousness'. To achieve wholeness he must perceive the unconscious as part of his totality. It is the process of integrating the unconscious that constitutes his journey; it is the very real risk of being overwhelmed by the unconscious that constitutes the danger of which all the myths warn him. For 'experience of the Self is always a defeat for the ego'.

The 'hero' who sets off on the journey of individuation has certain inescapable experiences before him. He must 'go down' into the unconscious — that is to say regress to infancy and the power of the mother. He must go, but he must also return. In

8 *The Integration of the Personality*, p. 3.

the process of making this journey he undergoes an encounter with the numinous. He will pass beyond his own unconscious into the collective unconscious where he will encounter the archetypes — the deepest compulsions of the human spirit, so fascinating and powerful that man's longing is to surrender his freedom to them as Ulysses longed to surrender to the Sirens. These compulsions both give life its whole purpose and meaning and also constitute the chief danger. Man's task in the process of becoming individuated is to learn both how to draw life from these powerful springs, but also to move in a free pattern that is his own making. Many of the great myths of love — Tristan and Isolde, Paolo and Francesca, Romeo and Juliet, Lancelot and Guinevere — show men and women caught in archetypal situations as helplessly as flies in a spider's web. They do not love; they are impaled upon their loving.

If we think of Ulysses in contrast to the love-myths, we see something much closer to life as it is normally experienced. Ulysses is caught in what is probably an incest-situation with Calypso, he is again caught and held by Circe, as well as being threatened by the Sirens, and he suffers other forms of imprisonment and innumerable dangers from every direction. He goes down into the underworld. But again and again he frees himself in order to continue with his journey. The archetypes both shape the journey (and Ulysses himself), but in the end he moves freely of them, and returns to Ithaca to inhabit the kingdom which is his own.

Jung suggests that Christ is the archetypal hero, living out the descent into the underworld which reconciles conscious and unconscious, after experiencing the impossibility of the opposites in the agony of crucifixion. The hero has his goal — in Christ's case 'the kingdom', in other cases 'the precious object hard to attain' (treasure, virgin, life potion, conquest of death, etc.) and these are to be found in regions of danger — water, the abyss, cave, forest, island, castle, etc.

The fear of the descent to Hades is at bottom the timidity and the resistance experienced by every natural person when it comes to delving too deeply in himself. If he experienced the sense of resistance alone, it would not be such a serious matter. But the psychic substratum, that dark realm of the un-known, actually exercises a fascinating attraction that threatens to become the more overpowering the further he advances into it.[9]

Given so much fear, so much understandable reluctance, what is it that can persuade the hero (the man bound upon indi-viduation) to embark on his fateful journey? The answer is that something happens to him. 'The meaning of my life', says Jung, 'is that life has addressed a question to me. Or, conversely, I myself am a question which is addressed to the world, and I must communicate my answer.'[10] Or, putting it another way 'the ego becomes aware of a polarity superordinate to itself.'[11]

'Dealing with the unconscious has become a question of life for us. It is a matter of spiritual being or non-being. All those who have met with the experience . . . know that the treasure lies in the depth of the water and will try to salvage it.[12] Men find themselves moved in ways that they do not and cannot under-stand in a direction that to them beckons with a sense of healing and completion. 'It is beyond all measure strange to conscious-ness and can find entrance into it only with the greatest difficul-ties.'

Certain symbols mark the individuation process. The symbol of wholeness is the circle, or mandala, and this may appear in dreams, fantasies, or drawings, of people who are very far from wholeness, though they will then recur in different forms as their lives go on. Other symbols — the rose, the tree, the child, will also make themselves known in dreams.

Undoubtedly those who embark upon the individuation pro-cess have an experience analogous to the 'going down' of the hero into the underworld, or Christ's descent into hell. In a sense everyone knows this, and knows also the danger involved, and this accounts for the common horror of introspection, and per-haps for some of the contempt sometimes reaped by psycho-analysis.

9 Ibid., p. 244.
10 *Memories, Dreams, Reflections,* p. 350.
11 Ibid., p. 378.
12 *The Integration of the Personality,* p. 72.

People generally believe that whoever descends into the unconscious lands himself in the oppressive confinement of egocentric subjectivity, and exposes himself in this blind alley to the attack of all the ferocious beasts the cavern of the psychic underworld is supposed to harbour.

The man who looks into the mirror of the waters does, indeed, see his own face first of all. Whoever goes to himself risks a confrontation with himself . . . This confrontation is the first test of courage on the inner way, a test sufficient to frighten off most people.[13]

What then? According to Jung, the extraordinarily painful experience of meeting one's 'shadow'. The Jungian 'shadow' is the side of oneself that one would rather not see or be aware of. It is the side which all one's life one has repressed in order to be the 'good' person that one is. The 'better' one is, the larger and more threatening one's shadow will be. In the course of the descent into the unconscious we discover the side of ourselves that we never permitted to develop, but which nevertheless is there, contributing more than we guess to our personality. This meeting is no light matter. 'The meeting with oneself is the meeting with one's own shadow. The shadow is a tight pass, a narrow door, whose painful constriction is spared to no one who climbs down into the deep wellspring. But one must learn to know oneself in order to know who one is.'[14]

Alongside the discovery that we are not what we seem is the parallel that others are not the devils we thought them. One particular projection gets withdrawn. 'The figure of the devil, in particular, is a most valuable and acceptable psychic possession, for as long as he goes about outside in the form of a roaring lion, we know where evil lurks.'[15] The terrible discovery in the realm of the unconscious is that the devil is not 'out there' but within us.

What comes next on the journey is something still more formless, and perhaps obscurely more frightening. 'What comes after the door is, surprising enough, a boundless expanse full of un-

13 Ibid., p. 69.
14 Ibid., p. 70.
15 Ibid., p. 69.

precedented uncertainty, with apparently no inside and no outside, no above and no below, no here and no there, no mine and
no thine, no good and no bad. It is the world of water . . .[16] We
have moved out of what seemed to be a capsulated, personal
system into the ocean of life itself. From this ever-flowing tide
we came, via our mother, into being and consciousness.'

In the descent into unconsciousness we again regress to the
mother, since only thus can we obtain freedom from her, in the
full emancipation that differentiation demands. This new encounter with the mother is fraught with danger. Theseus, in his
descent into the underworld, found himself merging with the
rocks. We can easily get sucked back into the landscape from
which, so precariously, our individual selves struggled to
consciousness. Other accounts of the underworld describe witches
such as Hecate, goddesses with a dark aspect such as Persephone,
devouring women. These symbolise the negative aspects of the
mother — chastising, imprisoning, devouring. Or again, she may
be present as the dragon whom the hero has to kill, in the knowledge that if he does not kill her, she will kill him. Beowulf
struggles with the gigantic, cruel figure of Grendel's mother
actually under the water, and makes the discovery that the sword
which previously has always stood him in good stead will not
work in this instance.

The dangers of the mother do not lie only in the images of her
as fierce and powerful, nor in the incestuous tie which underlies
such images. They lie also in the longing for inertia, in the wish
to sink back into a lotus-eating state of living death, in which no
demands would be made upon us, and in which we would never
be conscious enough to suffer strife and the pain it brings.

But in spite of the deep human awareness of the dangers of the
unconscious, men have repeatedly seen the need of the inner
journey. Religions have preached the descent as the only way to
the autonomy which is freedom and healing.

Jesus said unto him 'Except a man be born again, he cannot
see the kingdom of God.'
    Nicodemus saith unto him 'How can a man be born when
he is old? Can he enter the second time into his mother's

16 Ibid., p. 70.

womb, and be born?' Jesus answered 'Verily, verily, I say unto thee. Except a man be born of water and of the Spirit, he cannot enter into the Kingdom of God.[17]

The symbol of birth and of deliverance from the mother and all that she stands for in terms of peace, seduction, nourishment, points the way to the perpetual struggle waged by the adult man between ego-consciousness and the unconscious. Consciousness is a late development and as such it is precarious. Primitive man lived in fear of the state of possession by unconscious contents, and all man's striving, in his primitive phase, was towards the fortification of consciousness. Rituals and dogmas were part of this fortification. 'Dogma', says Jung, 'advises us not to have an unconscious.'[18]

The primitive fear of being consumed by the unconscious is expressed in many stories resembling that of Jonah and the whale in which the hero is swallowed up into the darkness of a big fish or monster, but because he *is* the hero, and carries man's hopes of increased consciousness, he not only gets out alive, but often in some sense victorious, bringing a piece of the fish with him.

The hero is important because he follows the voice inside him that demands his obedience in the quest of greater awareness. 'The hero, leader and saviour is also the one who discovers a new way to a greater certainty. Everything could be left as it was if this new way did not absolutely demand to be discovered, and did not visit humanity with all the plagues of Egypt until it is found. The undiscovered way is like something of the psyche that is alive.'[19]

What we scarcely know about, of course, are those who do not succeed in their quests, since these do not achieve the necessary growth in human consciousness, and do not become heroes. They may simply die in the attempt, by means of possession, or sloth, or by a paralysing longing for the past. 'It is', says Jung, 'tragic that the demon of the inner voice should spell greatest danger and indispensable help at the same time.'[20] Yet 'the integration

---

[17] St. John 3: 3–5.
[18] *The Integration of the Personality*, p. 60.
[19] Ibid., p. 305.
[20] Ibid., p. 304.

of the personality waits upon a challenge which, willingly, or unwillingly, we offer to ourselves'.[21]

How do men face and overcome such dangers? By the custom, time-honoured in most religions, and reappearing in somewhat different form in the field of psycho-analysis, of 'finding their guru'. Experience of the phenomena of the unconscious, sympathy, wisdom, detachment, make it possible for one human being to support another while integration of the unconscious is taking place. 'The patient needs the doctor, the *directeur de conscience*, while the eruption of the unconscious is going on or he may fall a prey to panic inspired by the overwhelming strangeness of his vision.' People 'need to feel a certain understanding and sympathy, perhaps even a certainty that they can share their crazy ideas with someone. This relieves them of the fear of capsizing.'[22]

What is clear is that the path of individuation is attended by suffering. This is partly the obvious suffering of loneliness, fear, uncertainty, insecurity, which must afflict anyone who embarks upon a psychic journey into unknown country just as it would afflict a traveller into unchartered hinterland. But it goes beyond this. The hero suffers because suffering is the only way in which he can perceive his goal. The awareness of the 'shadow' 'causes a cleavage and a tension of opposites which seek compensation in unity'. This conflict must strain the psyche to the utmost to the point where, half consciously, half unconsciously, it produces its answer, the answer of wholeness. With our reluctance to endure this painful conflict most of us opt out long before this happens. We seek to dodge it by pursuing a perfection which will allow us to deny the parts of our personality which make us uneasy. But individuation is not about perfection, but about wholeness, completeness, and nothing may be left out of this reckoning. 'To round itself out, life calls, not for perfection, but for completeness. For this the "barb in the flesh" is needed, the suffering of imperfection without which there is no forward or upward.'[23] Not only the suffering of imperfection, but mistakes, follies, stumbles.

[21] Ibid., p. 32.
[22] Ibid., p. 43.
[23] C. G. Jung, *Psychology and Alchemy: Collected Works*, Vol. 12 (Routledge & Kegan Paul, 1953), p. 208.

When one follows the path of individuation, when one lives one's own life, one must take mistakes into the bargain; life would not be complete without them. There is no guarantee — not for a single moment — that we will not fall into error or stumble into deadly peril. We may think there is a sure road. But that would be the road of death . . . Anyone who takes the sure road is as good as dead.[24]

Even religion, which has often been proclaimed as a sure road, is ambiguous here, as the fate of the Pharisees might have warned us. 'Woe to them who use religion as a substitute for another side of the life of the soul; they are in error and will be accursed. Religion is no substitute, but is to be added to the other activity of the soul as a completion. Out of the fullness of life shall you bring forth your religion; only then will you be blessed.'[25]

At the heart of Jung's individuation process lies a personal agony which cannot be dodged or avoided. The individual to whom it happens, pulled in different directions, suffering a condition in which he is asked to reconcile irreconcilable things, and suffering it, initially, by his own choice, feels that he is undergoing a crucifixion. He is not caught only between the opposites. Caught between conscious and unconscious, he dies a death as the unbalanced, unaware person that he was. Feeling his way painfully by symbols — mandala symbols, cross symbols, symbols of quaternity — he stumbles towards unity, the unity of wholeness.

The hitherto ignored unconscious, the 'lower part of man', has been admitted to the overt psychic life by an act of submission in which the ego-consciousness yielded supremacy to a superior totality. Such a submission means the recognition that man has two sides of such equal importance that they cannot become reconciled; their conflict has to be suffered. The cross of the quaternity is unavoidable and indispensable if we are to continue our pilgrimage through life.[26]

Sometimes Jung talks as if this descent into the unconscious,

[24] *Memories, Dreams and Reflections*, p. 328.
[25] *The Integration of the Personality*, p. 186.
[26] Ibid., p. 49.

there to suffer in the darkness this ultimate moment of self-surrender, is a once-for-all process to the individual to whom it happens. But elsewhere he suggests that what happens to the individual is only a microcosm of what, in fact, is the pattern of the universe. Death and resurrection are present in every moment and every experience of our lives, and thus we shall come across it in small things as in great. We shall return often from the underworld, sometimes bearing small, though precious jewels, at other times, and more rarely, having undergone archetypal experiences of a profundity which will change the course of our lives in major ways.

The hero's sense of vocation is closely connected with what Jung calls the 'anima', the feminine principle which leads him into growth and adventure as Beatrice led Dante on to make his spiritual pilgrimage. There can be no development without this feminine component (masculine in the case of a woman, and called the 'animus'), and where it is not projected on to an actual woman, who becomes the inspirer of the quest, and the interlocutor about it, then it is still experienced dynamically in the form of moods, reactions and impulses which shape the psychic life. It is not consciousness, but it is what produces consciousness. It is the 'lady' to whom every quest and every journey ought to be dedicated, since she is the 'onlie begetter' of the creative movement out of sloth and into psychic adventure. Without her there would be no incentive. 'The anima', says Jung, 'is a factor.'

'Anima' is the Latin for soul, and 'soul' says Jung, 'is the living in man, that which lives of itself and causes life'.[27]

What is the alternative to the hero's setting forth? There are not many people who strike us as heroes at all, using heroes in the rather special sense of someone prepared to adventure alone into the realm of the spirit. Not many really want to be chosen, to 'leave' as the New Testament says 'father and mother for my sake and for the gospel's' and Jung suggests that perhaps no one should leave father and mother in the psychic sense until they reach the point where they cannot help themselves. The hero needs to be compelled upon his journey, though the compulsion comes from within him. If he is to survive then he needs to have learned something of paradox if he is to keep his head among the bewildering opposites of the psyche. He needs to have some

27 Ibid.

inkling of the numinous and of the vast steppes of the unconscious. He 'should not be surprised if the empirical manifestations of unconscious contents bear the traits of boundlessness and indeterminability in space and time. In all times and places this is the quality of the numen and is, therefore, alarming to a careful consciousness that knows the value of precisely delimited concepts.[28]

What of those who do not undertake the quest? Some know well of its existence but manage to hold it in the mind as a theory, and so not to give themselves up without remainder to its fulfilment. Some dodge it out of horror of its implications. 'Some will quite heedlessly pass by the abyss of the Dionysiac secret and seize upon the rational, Darwinistic element to save themselves from mystic exaltation.'[29]

But the majority of people have no such inklings. They are not called, or they do not recognise the call. For them a resting-place lies in the conventions — moral, social, political, philosophic or religious. The enormous success of the conventions, Jung points out, stems from the fact that most men have neither will nor capacity to choose their own way. The conventions are 'a flight from the final consequences of one's own being'[30] and since few of us can manage 'being' most of the time it suits us very well. But what Jung calls 'true personality' behaves rather differently.

True personality always has vocation and believes in it, has fidelity to it as to God ... The greatness of historical personalities sufficiently explains why growth has never consisted in their unconditional subjection to convention, but, on the contrary, in their liberating freedom from convention. They thrust themselves up like mountain peaks out of the mass that clung to its collective fears, convictions, laws and methods, and chose their own way. ... A small and steep path that leads to the unknown.[31]

The conflict between collectivity and the individual, between society and 'personality' has been waged unendingly in history,

[28] Ibid., p. 177.
[29] Ibid., 155.
[30] Ibid., p. 290.
[31] Ibid., p. 290, 291.

but there are signs that in our own time the battle is becoming more intense because the pressure of the collective has become more unrelenting. This makes new demands on consciousness, demands which we have answered inadequately.

It seems as if the building up of collective life and the unprecedented massing together of men, so characteristic of our time, were needed to make the individual aware of the fact that he was being strangled in the meshes of the organised mob. The collectivism of the medieval church seldom exerted sufficient pressure on the individual to turn his relation to society into a universal problem. So this question, also, remained undeveloped, at the level of projection; and the task of infusing into it at least a germ of consciousness, albeit under the mask of a neurotic individualism, was left to our own day.[32]

If we accept that some individuals in our own day are likely to feel called to this journey out of the morass of the collective, and into the integration of ego and unconscious which Jung regarded as the *unio mystica*, then what form does the hero's journey take nowadays?

Jolande Jacobi sets the stages out in some detail in her book *The Way of Individuation*. To begin with she sees two kinds of individuation, one a natural phenomenon, the other an *opus contra naturam*, as man moves out of his inertia, compelled by a vision that demands more than natural satisfactions. The two forms, as she sees them, are as different as a wild fruit from a cultivated one.

So far as the natural form is concerned, there is a sort of movement towards maturity which no human being can completely avoid.

Like a seed growing into a tree, life unfolds stage by stage. Triumphant ascent, collapse, crises, failures, and new beginnings strew the way. It is the path trodden by the great majority of mankind, as a rule unreflectingly, unconsciously, unsuspectingly, following its labyrinthine windings from birth to death in hope and longing. It is hedged about with struggle and suffering, joy and sorrow, guilt and error, and nowhere is

[32] Ibid., p. 271.

there security from catastrophe. For as soon as a man tries to escape every risk and prefers to experience life only in his head, in the form of ideas and fantasies, as soon as he surrenders to opinions of 'how it ought to be' and, in order not to make a false step, imitates others whenever possible, he forfeits the chance of his own independent development.[33]

The natural kind of individuation is largely unconscious, but there are those who, because of their courage in flinging themselves into life, and experiencing it as completely as they can, do achieve wholeness and wisdom.

The other form of individuation involves conscious experience of the fact. The Jungian form of analysis sees it — the complete and comprehensive development of the personality — as its goal, and though most Jungians would not regard analysis as a *sine qua non*, they would regard it as a tool finely designed to help in this process. The work of analysis aims to strengthen consciousness so that it will be equal to the 'quest of the hero', but it does not allow consciousness to become dictator. At every point attention must be paid to the unconscious and the 'messages' it sends.

The polarity of conscious and unconscious have their analogy in the first and second halves of the human life-span. The first half of human life has as its goal the establishing of ourselves in the world — we learn what kind of world it is we live in, how to exist tolerably alongside others, how to find outlets for our talents, ambition, sexuality. This is not only an analogy for ego-consciousness; we cannot adjust to the world satisfactorily without developing ego-strength. The second half of life has a different set of aims and duties. The zenith of life is passed, and men and women gradually become aware of the reality of death, as well as the process of ageing. They see what they have missed and still have time to achieve, as well as what has been irretrievably lost. A kind of crisis occurs.

To look such truths in the eye [says Dr. Jacobi] is a test of courage. It demands insight into the necessity of growing old, and the courage to renounce what is no longer compatible with it. For only when one is able to discriminate between what

[33] Jolande Jacobi, *The Way of Individuation* (Hodder and Stoughton, 1967), p. 16.

must be discarded and what still remains as a valuable task for the future will one also be able to decide whether one is ready to strike out in the new direction consciously and positively.[34]

If this task is dodged then neurosis is likely to occur, but even those who tackle the human task faithfully are liable to serious crises of one sort or another — illness, divorce, change of job, etc. — as they enter the second half of life, and this may be absolutely necessary for their eventual achievement of wholeness. For 'whereas the first half of life is, in the nature of things, governed and determined by expansion and adaptation to outer reality, the second is governed by restriction or reduction to the essential, by adaptation to the inner reality'.[35]

What is happening is a change of centre, as a man becomes aware of a wholeness of which his little ego is but a part, though a crucial part. He obtains a glimpse of what Jung calls 'the Self', 'that transconscious, central authority of the psyche, which seems from the beginning to be in *a priori* possession of the goal, and, with a kind of fore-knowledge, aims at the entelechy, the unity and wholeness of the human personality'. Jung has movingly described the movement of the unconscious around the Self, like a planet around the sun.

We can hardly avoid the impression that the unconscious process moves in a spiral path around a 'centre' that it slowly approaches, the 'properties' of the 'centre', meanwhile, showing themselves always more clearly. We could also put it the other way round and say that the central point, knowable in itself, acts like a magnet upon the disparate materials and processes of the unconscious and, like a crystal grating, catches them one by one ... It seems as if the personal complications and the dramatic, subjective climaxes that make up the quintessence of life and its whole intensity were but hesitation or timid shrinking before the finality of this strange or uncanny process of crystallization ... One often has the impression that the personal psyche chases around this centre like a shy animal, fascinated and frightened at the same time, always running away and yet always approaching.[36]

34 Ibid., p. 22.   35 Ibid., p. 25.
36 *The Integration of the Personality*, p. 197.

Dr. Jacobi traces the developments of the personality which
lead into the individuation process. In youth a certain one-
sidedness in development provides the spur for activity which
makes it possible for establishment in the world. Some of the
functions of consciousness — thinking, feeling, sensation, intuition — will predominate over the others, as will an introverted or extraverted attitude to life. The predominant attitude
and function will help produce the 'persona', the 'face' which one
shows the world, and which is necessary if a man is to be accepted
in the world.

Side by side with the ego, however, we develop the 'shadow',
the sum of all the qualities repressed or unlived as the ego
developed. And beyond the personal shadow lies the collective
shadow, the sum of all the qualities which mankind has collectively rejected. In either case the shadow tends to be projected
upon others — in the case of the individual upon our acquaintance, in the case of society, upon unpopular races or social groups.

The individuation process demands the taking back of these
projections. 'We learn by experience, mostly unpleasant, through
collisions of all kinds, through disappointments and illnesses,
that we as much as other people have shadow qualities.'

Another sort of projection involved is that upon the man or
woman. Instead of projecting the animus or anima upon the man
or woman in the outer world, and so falling in love with them,
those upon the path of individuation have to learn to recognise
that what they find irresistibly fascinating in the other is their
own contrasexual element projected. Dr. Jacobi points out the
difference there is between the kind of man/woman relationship
that is dominant in the first half of life, and the kind (within the
individual) which may occur in the second. 'If the "bodily child"
is born of the first form of relationship, the fruit of the second
is the "spiritual child".[37] When we can bear to discover and
welcome the fact that we are female as well as male, or male as
well as female, then birth occurs in the psyche.'

As the opus proceeds a man discovers that he has begun to see
his own problems from a different perspective. 'It becomes possible for him to see his apparently insurmountable personal
problems in the light of objective problems common to all human-

[37] *The Way of Individuation*, p. 45.

ity, and this not infrequently robs them of their urgency and their sting.'[38]

Yet he has difficulties of another sort. He is 'in the underworld' of which the myths and fairy-tales speak, and there he finds himself confronting archetypal figures of a deep numinosity. 'The archetypal material that comes up', says Dr. Jacobi, 'is the same as that of which the delusions of the insane are composed. The shattering effect of the borderline phenomena of these inner experiences and confrontations brings about a transformation which enables the matured personality to take the "middle way" and finally win to psychic peace.'[39]

Through all these immense labours, with all their pains and crises in the day-to-day living of the person involved, the individual is moving towards (and at the behest of) the Self. 'The Self', says Jung, 'then functions as a union of opposites and thus constitutes the most immediate experience of the Divine which it is psychologically possible to imagine.'[40]

Dr. Jacobi adds 'it represents the unity in which all psychic opposites cancel out'.

The Self, in Jungian psychology, is not God, but may be seen as a reflection of God, dwelling within the human heart. It is 'that vital centre in the psyche which possesses the greatest charge of energy. Every content that is anywhere near this supercharged centre receives from it a numinous power, as though "possessed" by it. Again and again man has experienced that from this centre he could sense God's workings in his psyche at their most overwhelming.'[41] When he places something other than God in this centre he is apt to become a victim of his own destruction. In *Mysterium Coniunctionis* Jung quotes the alchemical saying 'God is an infinite circle (or sphere) whose centre is everywhere and circumference nowhere'.

By such experience man is led into transformation, though 'every individuation process consists of a chain of transformations'.

Jung also applied his ideas about individual development in the context of societies. He felt that Western society had valued

[38] Ibid., pp. 46, 47.
[39] Ibid.
[40] C. G. Jung, *Psychology and Religion: Collected Works*, Vol. 11 (Routledge & Kegan Paul, 1958).
[41] *The Way of Individuation*, p. 54.

ego-consciousness at the expense of the message of the unconscious and that this was systematically cutting men off from
God and from the instincts, and leading steadily towards despair
and neurosis.

Protestantism, with its emphasis upon reason at the expense
of man's intuitive, emotional, irrational side, had underlined the
poverty of man when he tries to deny his roots. In his desperation
man seeks for 'good' everywhere but in his own psyche. 'The
psyche has little by little become that Nazareth from which nothing
good can come; and for this reason people seek it in the four
corners of the world, the farther off and the more out of the way
the better.' And 'Everything that presented him (Protestant man)
with no thought-content has been torn from him. If now he
should go and cover his nakedness with the gorgeous dress of the
Orient, like the theosophists, he would be untrue to his own
history.'[42]

Yet possibly, in his dire poverty, thinks Jung, man may turn to
rediscover his true nature. His terrible indigence will describe
its own cure. 'It is dangerous to confess to spiritual poverty, for
whoever is poor has cravings and whoever craves draws his fate
upon himself.'[43] The danger is the contact with the living God
whom man has so assiduously fled. 'When God is nearest the
danger is greatest.'

Jung sees the Church as standing in an ambivalent relationship
to man's struggles to reach, or avoid, God. Though it believes
itself as existing to help man find the road to God, it equally, and
in a sense, necessarily, exists to protect him from the dangers of
being overwhelmed by the experience of God. Dogma anaesthe-
tises the mind against the agony of first-hand experience of its
truth. Ritual sedates the believer against the incursion of archetypal content, and saves him from possession by them. The
symbolism of the Mass, for all its potential dynamic, lulls him in
a cradle of tradition, in which he need never awaken. In extreme cases, this holding operation of the Church can save its
members from the insanity which could come from an accidental
falling into the hands of the living God, as Jung explains in the
case of Nicholas of Flue.

[42] *The Integration of the Personality*, p. 63.
[43] Ibid., p. 64.

It (the dogmatic symbol) protects a person from a direct experience of God as long as he does not mischievously expose himself. But if, like Brother Nick, he leaves home and family, lives too long alone and gazes too deeply into the dark mirror, then the awful event of the meeting may befall him. Yet even then the traditional symbol, come to full flower through the centuries, may operate like a healing draught and divert the fatal incursion of the living godhead into the hallowed spaces of the Church.'[44]

Part of the Church's ambivalence lies in the way that it has encouraged Christians, for two thousand years, to identify only with the light, 'good', side of themselves, and thus to deny the dark, 'bad' side. If the individuation theory in any way describes what happens to the man who is struggling towards maturity, then the Church has encouraged immaturity, since it has made it harder for its adherents to pass through the 'narrow door'; the agonising encounter with one's own shadow. And in Jungian theory, there can be no growth, no maturity, without this painful encounter. As individuals who have not encountered the shadow we are at the mercy of our projections — we are liable to see all around us, in our relatives, neighbours, colleagues, the 'badness' which we will not acknowledge within. This is deeply destructive, as the history of innumerable marriages can show, but when the same blindness occurs in the society made up of these individuals then the result is no less than total catastrophe — the catastrophe of racialism, genocide, war.

If we are to find a way through this terrifying impasse, then we must do what our whole European Christian heritage makes it hard for us to do, and face the *equivalence* of good and evil both within ourselves and within our society. We are neither good nor bad, but ideally we should stand at the point of balance between these two opposites, and this is what makes it possible to escape them. This is the only way they can be reconciled and mankind's torment can be eased. The Devil, in some sense, must be put back into the godhead (Jung suggests that what we have taken for a Trinity may in reality be a Quaternity) if he is not to wield the almost unlimited power he enjoys because of our unconsciousness.

[44] Ibid., p. 59.

To pursue this quest of consciousness, to be the hero, whether for nation or individual, costs 'no less than everything'. One writer uses the story of the healing of the man sick of the palsy as an illustration of it. 'The affirmation of the margin of freedom, however tiny, whereby a man can move from his bed, from his neurotic determinism, into action. This action . . . is not sacrifice at the temple for the appeasing of a terrible God, nor is it in terms of a mediator doing it. The sacrifice is inner and personal.[45] And again:

> The individual way, involving conflicts with the orthodox and with the collective, suffering rejection by the collective, and a final willingness to meet crucifixion. . . . The willingness to go the individual way and to manifest God in reality against all the un-God-like collective elements, so that there must inevitably be terrific conflict. And if one follows it to its fulfilment, it is bound to lead to an even deeper death . . . it involves the individual having taken upon himself the pursuit of the opposites; which includes both dark and light within.[46]

Mankind, whatever his religious belief or lack of it, is called into transformation, a transformation towards which he puts up a huge resistance.

It is far more dramatic, exciting and alluring to stay in a *participation mystique* with the unconcious archetypes, to 'feel' the Christ, have dreams even that move us, and not really be changed. But if we truly relate to and dis-identify with the archetype, living it only in its limited, mortal aspect, we are in process of transformation.[47]

[45] Elizabeth B. Howes, 'Son of Man — Image of the Self' (Guild of Pastoral Psychology Lecture).
[46] Ibid.
[47] Ibid.

CHAPTER THREE

The Fabulous Journey

MAN IS A JOURNEYING CREATURE, AND IT IS NOT SURPRISING, therefore, that literature is full of man's struggles towards inner progress from simple folk-tales such as *The Sleeping Beauty, The Golden Goose,* or *Beauty and the Beast,* down to contemporary attempts to express journey like *The Cocktail Party* or *The Lord of the Rings.*

Certain threads play an important part in the design of stories of quest and journey. They are not universal, but they are sufficiently common (in stories widely separated in time, culture and place) to be worth noticing. When man tries to describe what his life is like he mentions certain kinds of experience with an almost monotonous regularity.

Some of those experiences would be predictable even without knowledge of the *milieu* from which they sprang. There is a certain obviousness about human life which is inescapable. All men are born and die, they form emotional relationships with those around them, they have a need to establish their identity in 'the world', they have sexual desires, they are afraid of pain, illness, suffering, old age and death.

Inevitably this simple, 'natural', progression is mirrored in folk-tales and in art.

Yet buried, with artless art, even in early and unsophisticated attempts at describing the human predicament, is a knowledge that life is somehow more mysterious than appears on the surface. Folk-tales know, and do not know; they imply but they do not explain. Thus, *The Sleeping Beauty,* an apparently simple story, tells us and does not tell us. We may read it as a simple story, or we may sense that it *could* be saying something about virginity and its defences, and how those defences may be breached. It never commits the mistake of spelling out what it means, or actually drawing its readers' attention to what their deep fears or longings may be, and it is not likely that the originator of the tale was capable of such a thing. It was unpretentious, innocent, and 'only a story', so that no one can possibly take offence.

The parabolic nature of these simple quest stories means not only that the meaning may be hidden, but that several different meanings can be read at once. The story can present a different face according to the intelligence and perception of its audience. Thus, in the story of *The Golden Goose*, the third son of the woodcutter sets off on an errand, and, because he shares his meagre food and drink with an old woman he meets on the road, he finds the golden goose and is saved from poverty and ignominy. On a shrewd peasant level the story is about a form of insurance — if you are hard-up and often hungry you can't afford to make enemies because you never know when you'll need a helping hand. On a simple psychological level the story says that love and a generous attitude breed kindness in return. But on another level still the story seems to be feeling for a much more mysterious observation about life — that if we are prepared to give whatever we have without reserve then we may get an almost absurdly generous return for our pains — a golden goose.

Other folk-tales also struggle to express the transforming moment — the moment when a situation of despair becomes one of hope and joy. In a world such as that of the folk-tales where causation is of little interest, the word for this is 'magic'. 'Magic' stops us asking 'How?'. So, the frog who so repulsed the princess when he was a fellow-diner and bedfellow can become a prince without our asking awkward questions. The Beast, whose heartbreak caused Beauty to forsake her father for the second time and by her own choice, is transformed into a personable husband. The Prince can reach the Sleeping Beauty through an impassable hedge of briars and wake her from the death-in-life that enthrals her.

As folk-tales pass into high art the sense of mystery often becomes more explicit. Those who retell the stories are less interested in the narrative itself than in the opportunity it lends to discuss the human lot with its share of success and failure, suffering and joy. Yet the deepest emotions may still remain as it were 'buried' in the text, known and unknown by their author. Sophocles never directly recognises the universal human conflict to which his play *Oedipus Rex* gives expression. Instead, Thebes is gripped in a mood of death and despair, an atmosphere in which there can be no growth. The city's affliction is to be caught in a tide of death from which there is no escaping—

> Death in the fruitful flowering of her soil;
> Death in the pastures.[1]

Dimly the wisest among the Thebans perceives the root of the trouble.

> There is an unclean thing,
> Born and nursed in our soil, polluting our soil,
> Which must be driven away, not kept to destroy us.

The scene is thus set for one of the most terrible expositions of man's path of suffering in the whole of literature.

Oedipus is viewed entirely through the dark glass of the tragic vision. When we move into the romantic vein of *Beowulf* or *Tristan* or the Grail legend, or into the ironic vein of Apuleius (whose hero Lucius is forced to make his painful quest disguised as an ass) then we become aware of how rich and various are the pathways of the inner journey, and how men may construe the same bitter and glorious experiences in very different ways.

The heroic stories are marked by certain inescapable details. Outstanding among these is the strong masculinity of the hero or traveller as he sets out on his adventures. It is not just that the traveller is never a woman (women are the inspirers of quest, like Beatrice, or the innumerable maidens of Arthurian legend; or they are influential goddesses like Athene, or life-givers like Apuleius' Isis; or they are temptresses like Circe and the Sirens; or they are merciless devourers like Ishtar in the Gilgamesh myth). The hero is not just a man; he is a man who has proved his strength in battle, and is ready to attempt more daring and unusual feats than most men will attempt. Odysseus has more than proved himself on the plains of Troy before the fateful journey home to Ithaca begins. He is an adept at fighting, at intrigue, at disguises. He has a better chance of survival in dangerous con-

[1] Sophocles, *Oedipus Rex*, tr. E. F. Watling (Penguin, 1947).

ditions than an ordinary man would have. But first he has to extricate himself from the painful situation of his imprisonment by Calypso, whom it is tempting to identify as the mother. He is the 'unwilling lover of a willing lady', and he mourns perpetually for the freedom which at length is granted to him. The journey begins.

Beowulf is a man of undisputed might before he faces the terrible challenge of the devilish monster Grendel. He is well-born, stalwart, and 'the strongest of living men'. He has 'the strength of thirty men in the grip of his hand', in fact he is so strong that swords are apt to splinter beneath him when he uses them in battle. In his youth he has destroyed 'an entire family of giants', not to mention a number of sea-monsters, and in boyhood he had, just for fun, embarked on a desperate enterprise with his friend Breca 'to chance our lives at sea. This we did. While swimming, each carried a naked sword in hand to defend ourselves against whales. ... We stayed together for five nights until a storm drove us apart; a tempestuous sea, the most bitter weather, nightfall and the north wind, turned savagely against us.' But Beowulf survived all this and can remark comfortably 'Fortune is apt to favour the man who keeps his nerve.'[2]

Like many another hero, Beowulf makes his bow on the public stage, in the manner of the boy David, at a moment when everyone is looking for a champion who is not afraid to take on impossible odds. Similarly, Tristan, another fearless and accomplished soldier, offers himself as a champion to face Morholt who demands the terrible tribute of Cornish men and girls to be shipped to Ireland as slaves. The hero is apt to offer his life for the people, and by taking the risk, and backing it with his unusual strength and skill, freeing them from unspeakable bondage.

Gilgamesh, the Sumerian hero, has an altogether more overweening kind of strength, which perhaps makes his eventual humbling by the journey all the more moving. 'Gilgamesh went on a long journey, was weary, worn-out with labour, and returning engraved on a stone the whole journey.'[3] But to start with he was a natural prince among men. 'When the gods created Gilgamesh they gave him a perfect body. Shamash the glorious sun endowed him with beauty, Adad the god of the storm endowed

[2] *Beowulf*, tr. David Wright (Penguin, 1957).
[3] *The Epic of Gilgamesh*, tr. N. K. Sandars (Penguin, 1970).

him with courage, the great gods made his beauty perfect, surpassing all others. Two thirds they made him god and one third man.' Not surprisingly, his contemporaries complain that 'his arrogance has no bounds by day or night'. He takes all the young men to war, and in addition 'his lust leaves no virgin to her lover'. Yet no one dreams of trying to check this arrogant tyrant. Rather, the gods deal with the situation themselves. They create for him a 'shadow', a brother who resembles him in looks, and is his equal in strength. The 'noble Enkidu' as he is called, is almost an animal, covered in matted hair, and 'innocent of mankind'. He eats grass with the gazelle and drinks with the wild beasts at the water-hole, until he is tamed by the 'woman's art' of a harlot. Enkidu and Gilgamesh meet and at once become locked in fierce combat. With difficulty Gilgamesh overcomes Enkidu and they become friends and inseparables. They embark together on a desperate enterprise, that of overcoming evil in the person of the giant Humbaba.

In the true manner of the hero Gilgamesh knows that it is his task to do what no man has been able to do before him. It is partly that he sees there is a need for it among those with whom he lives. 'Here in the city man lies oppressed at heart, man perishes with despair in his heart.' He is acutely aware of the danger he is about to undergo, yet sees no real choice before him. 'If this enterprise is not to be accomplished', he prays desperately to the Sun God, Shamash, 'why did you move me, with the restless desire to perform it?' Death is preferable to the dishonour of not attempting the brave deed. 'If I fall I leave behind me a name that endures; men will say of me, "Gilgamesh has fallen in fight with ferocious Humbaba".'

Who are the heroes? There is something ambivalent about their literary *persona* since they are both 'everyman' and also someone who has passed beyond the ordinary fears and temptations which bedevil a man and moved on to a new plane of living and experiencing. Whereas in folk-tales the hero who makes good is often, significantly, a poor or despised boy, essentially 'ordinary' in his nature, with whom the common folk might easily identify, in 'high art' he tends to be an aristocrat, or a super-aristocrat, divine parentage mixing with noble blood. So, in an almost biblical way, authors are careful to tell us who a man's forebears were. The story of Beowulf starts several generations before the hero himself so that his impeccable credentials can be established. Oedipus and Tristan and Lancelot were the children of kings, and Gilgamesh was the son of the goddess Ninsun.

Man's instinct for the importance of heredity, together with his snobbish fascination with 'what great ones do', are alike attracted by this glamorising of his heroes. The great ones may only, when it comes down to it, be doing what the rest of us do — striving to achieve and to conquer ungovernable fears, battling with powerful desires and infatuations, obeying mysterious vocations, struggling with the fear of pain and death — but their lordliness sharpens the tragedy, and their gigantic strength makes their eventual weakness the more poignant. Spirit does battle with flesh, conscious with unconscious. We are spellbound because we recognise our own conflict in the valour of the heroes, our own joy and agony projected upon a giant screen.

A recognition that, even for the aristocrats among the heroes, the initiation into life is not all silk hangings and delicately carved cradles, comes from the strong tradition of the hero as an orphan, either deprived early in life of one of his parents, or stolen from them, or actually abandoned by them. Tristan's mother, Blanchefleur, died in giving birth to him (hence the tragic implication of his name), and he was brought up by a tutor, Governal. The devoted tutor, a kind of father-surrogate, who teaches the hero the arts of war, is a recurring figure in myth. One of the most moving descriptions of him occurs in *The Iliad* in the description of teaching the young Odysseus. Lancelot was stolen from his parents in infancy. Galahad, it is always a faint surprise to remember, is a bastard, the son of Lancelot who, as a result of a trick, lay with Elaine, believing her to be Guinevere. He grows up apart from his father. The infant Oedipus was exposed on the mountain-side, his feet pinioned so that there would be no chance of survival and return to his parents.

A Jungian discussion of the Grail legend, and in particular the legend of the hero Perceval, examines the phenomenon of the orphan.[4]

Perhaps it is that with a fatherless boy all those conditions that dispose him to become a hero are strengthened and

[4] Emma Jung and M-L von Franz, *The Grail Legend* (Hodder and Stoughton, 1971).

intensified because he has to make his own way and is compelled to develop independence and feelings of responsibility, while a boy who lives under the guidance of a father who offers him support will be less impelled towards such achievements. While for the latter the father represents the figure of the 'successful man' outwardly, this image falls back upon the fatherless boy himself, so to speak, and drives him on to its realization. On the other hand it is possible that as a result of the father's absence — whether he be dead or simply not fulfilling his role as father and masculine example — there is engendered in the son the feeling of attitude that all possibilities and provinces of masculine achievement are open to him who can anticipate nothing from the father. . . . A further factor seems to be connected with the mother. A woman without a husband will naturally be inclined to transfer what she would have expected of him — that he be a hero, for instance — on to the son, in the hope that he will fulfil what the father was unable to achieve. The following curious fact also plays a part. In the dreams and fantasies of even happily married women, a mysteriously fascinating masculine figure often appears, a demonic or divine dream or shadow lover to which Jung has given the name of *animus*. Not uncommonly the woman cherishes a more or less conscious secret idea that one of her children, preferably the eldest or youngest, was fathered by this psychic lover. Superhuman powers will readily be attributed to such a child . . . The hero figure is one of those eternal, archetypal images which slumber in the depths of every soul and which determine human life and destiny in unexpected measure.

If to be fatherless is one of the characteristic features of the hero, it must be made clear that he is considered to be descended from either a superhuman or a nonhuman father instead of an ordinary human father . . . The stories in Greek mythology of a god, often in animal form, uniting with a human woman — Zeus for instance as a bull with Europa or as a swan with Leda are universally known. Demigods and heroes result from such unions. It is also well known that children frequently have the idea that they are not the offspring of their parents but were substituted or adopted by them; such a child feels that in reality he or she is probably either a prince or a princess. Such fantasies, even when not conscious, can have an influence on the behaviour of a child and may be the basic cause of an estrangement from reality and a lack of adaptation. These can of course be set aside simply as wish-fulfilment fantasies — which on the one hand they undoubtedly are; on the other, however, they possess a certain value. They serve to inspire courage in a young person who, face to face with the world, naturally feels small, weak, helpless and in its power; they help him to master his fear and uncertainty. Correctly understood this means that in the prototype of the hero an idea is personified which is an invaluable spur and an effective support in life ... This does not mean that he (the individual) thinks he is a hero but that he will conduct himself like one if the occasion arises. On a higher level than the mythological or the childish the same idea is expressed when the unknown father is considered as being a spiritual, divine being or principle. This idea is particularly clearly expressed in Christ, the son of God and man. It is evident that this concept means a great deal more than just a support in life or an infantile fantasy. It expresses in itself the fundamental and ineradicable feeling that something dwells in man which is more than purely human or animal, namely an immortal soul, a divine spark. ...

Perhaps because the hero is so often fatherless his relation to his mother tends to be a close one. The fatherless child is bereft at one blow of his rival, his exemplar (of manliness), and of his protector (against the overwhelming power of his mother's love as well as against the outer world). He is therefore likely to be more aware than most children of both the seductive and the devouring aspects of his mother's love. All male children endure this conflict to a greater or lesser degree, but it would not be surprising if, in the life-story of the orphaned hero, we could detect the signs of this epic struggle. Sure enough, devouring women, particularly in the form of goddesses, or half-goddesses, are not at all uncommon, and monsters or dragons who must be slain (often to save a virgin from destruction, as in the story of St. George) recur almost monotonously.

It is not only the hidden awareness of incest against which the hero (or child) struggles. In psychological terms the mother may be seen to stand for the unconscious. The child has to struggle out of this 'fairy-tale' world and move painfully in the direction of consciousness; the outer world will beckon to it alluringly and it will want to make this journey, but at times it will be overwhelmed with longing for the mother and the peace and inertia for which she stands. Man's mourning over the Fall, and his innumerable longings for a lost Paradise or golden age, recall this primordial experience. 'The development and preservation of ego consciousness is often represented by the hero myth, for it is an achievement that can be compared to a fight with an overwhelming monster and which calls for almost superhuman strength.'

The most frightening of the monsters which Beowulf fights is, in fact, female, and the mother of another terrible monster called Grendel. Not surprisingly the battle takes place deep in the waters of a lake i.e. in the unconscious, and it is a bloody and terrible conflict. Grendel's mother lives in 'an unvisited land among wolf-haunted hills, windswept crags and perilous fentracks, where mountain waterfalls disappear into mist and are lost underground.' In this lonely place Beowulf plunges into the lake where the monster is lurking.

The tumbling waters swallowed him up. It was the best part of a day before he saw the bottom of the lake. But it was not long before the ravening she-beast, who had lorded it for half a century in the waste of waters, realized that someone from above was exploring the monsters' home. She made a lunge and grabbed the hero with her loathsome claws, yet did not wound his body. The chainmail gave him such complete protection that she was unable to penetrate his closely-linked corslet with her horrible talons. When the she-wolf of the water reached the lake floor, she carried the prince off to her den in such a manner that in spite of his courage he was unable to wield his weapons. But swarms of weird beasts assaulted him in the depths, pursued him, and tore at his corslet with their ferocious tusks.

The contestants fight furiously together, Beowulf making the discovery that the fine sword he carries, tempered in many a battle, is of no use here. Finally, he kills the monster by striking her with a sword he finds in her den, but meanwhile those watching the lake from above and seeing it first convulsed, and then still and bloodstained, assume the worst and turn sorrowfully away.

Odysseus encounters the devouring woman rather differently. Significantly, the start of his journey is delayed by his long imprisonment with the nymph Calypso, and he is only released by the intervention of the gods. The peace, beauty and comfort of the life which surrounds Calypso speak eloquently of infantile memories of mother and home. Going to visit her, Hermes

came to a great cave, wherein dwelt the nymph of the braided tresses: and he found her within. And on the hearth there was a great fire burning, and from afar through the isle was smelt the fragrance of cleft cedar blazing, and of sandal wood. And the nymph within was singing with a sweet voice as she fared to and fro before the loom, and wove with a shuttle of gold. And round about the cave there was a wood blossoming, alder and poplar and sweet-smelling cypress . . . And lo, there about the hollow cave trailed a gadding garden vine, all rich with clusters. And fountains four set orderly were running with clear water . . . And all around soft meadows bloomed of violet and parsley.[5]

Amidst all this peace and plenty, however, Odysseus never ceases to mourn and to complain that his 'sweet life was ebbing away'. He sits gazing longingly out over the sea, 'straining his soul with tears and groans and griefs'.

Calypso's imprisonment of him works by the subtlest and least brutal means, and the most difficult aspect of it is that he can never hope to return the quality of the love she gives to him, since his thoughts are always turning to his journey. Later the Sirens demonstrate the devouring possibilities of women in more obvious form, as they enchant the hero with their song 'sitting in the meadow, and all about is a great heap of bones of men, corrupt in death, and round the bones the skin is wasting'.

Gilgamesh wrestles with the destructive quality of femininity in the person of the goddess Ishtar. Transfigured by victory, and

[5] *The Odyssey*, tr. Butcher & Lang (Macmillan, 1949).

in the full pride of his beauty and strength, he attracts her lust, a lust which has proved fatal in the case of her other human lovers each of whom has been terribly punished and broken. Bravely Gilgamesh reminds her of this pathetic train, and brings down her revenge upon the people of Uruk.

Ishtar is reminiscent of Circe, since she turns many of her lovers into animals, yet Circe, once she has been dominated by Odysseus, at once loses her destructive aspect and becomes a force for good in the story. She begins, simply enough, by recognising that Odysseus is worn out, physically and mentally, by the intolerable stresses of his journey. She offers rest, food, wine, love, a re-discovery of the body and its simple delights. But once Odysseus is rested and restored it is Circe who spurs him to the next and most terrible stage of his journey — to go down into Hades and confront the spirits of the dead, and in particular of the prophet Teiresias. At this description of the most crucial part of Odysseus' journey Circe refers to him as 'leader of the people'. The 'leader' must visit the prophet in order to be told 'the way and the measure of thy path'. In the course of the journey Odysseus also meets his own mother among the spirits. When he emerges from Hades it is Circe who meets him, who listens to his story, and who sends him forth upon the next stage of his journey, telling him how to outwit the Sirens and how to survive the ordeals ahead. Her function in Odysseus' life is partly one of tenderness, but it is also one of insight; she knows what awaits him and how to prepare for it as he cannot. It is a shock to realise that her role is the same as that of the virginal Beatrice; Dante found his inspiration in a higher, thinner atmosphere than did the Greeks. But for Odysseus, as perhaps for many who have followed, progress in the journey is rooted in a bodily experience, and warmth as well as insight is indispensable to its achievement. 'The gateway of the mysterious female' says the Chinese poet Lao Tzu 'is the root of heaven and earth.'

Gilgamesh has a parallel experience to that of Odysseus and Dante in his quest to find immortality.

Then follows the search for the ancestral wisdom [writes N. K. Sandars, an editor of Gilgamesh] which takes Gilgamesh to the limits of the earth as did Odysseus' journey to find Teiresias. This ... journey ... can be based on no historical event; the topography is otherworldly in a manner which before it was not. The planes of romantic and spiritual adventure have coalesced. Although clothed in the appearances of primitive geography it is a spiritual landscape as much as Dante's Dark Wood, Mountain and Pit.

Gilgamesh is also directed by a woman, a 'daughter of the Sun' (like Circe), called Siduri. Siduri is young and beautiful. 'Besides the sea she lives, the woman of the vine, the maker of wine; Siduri sits in the garden at the edge of the sea, with the golden bowl and the golden vats that the gods gave her.' She at once grasps the agony and the longing of his quest though she does not know its purpose. 'Why are your cheeks so starved and why is your face so drawn? Why is despair in your heart and your face like the face of one who has made a long journey? Yes, why is your face burned from heat and cold, and why do you come here wandering over the pastures in search of the wind?'

When Gilgamesh tries to describe to her the horror of death which sends him upon his journey, she tells him to go back and accept the ordinary, unquestioned lot of humanity. 'Let your clothes be fresh, bathe yourself in water, cherish the little child that holds your hand, and make your wife happy in your embrace; for this too is the lot of man.'

Gilgamesh insists, however, that this blind acceptance is of no use to him and, grudgingly, Siduri tells him that there is a faint hope, no more than that, that he may persuade Urshanabi, the ferryman of the gods, to take him across the waters of death into the land of immortality.

The role of women is of crucial importance in the myths of Gilgamesh and of Odysseus, but later in literature (I am, of course, talking about the West), we find women achieving a different sort of importance. It is deeply dyed with Christian idealism, it is strongly marked with guilt, and it struggles with an ambivalent attitude to sex, managing to describe it tenderly and be shocked about it at the same time. It is a far cry from Odysseus who seems totally unworried about Penelope's view of his adventures.

Denis de Rougement has written exhaustively about the way love in the West has become tragically, almost inextricably, entangled with the idea of adultery. He believes that we have an

unnatural obsession with obstacle in our loving. A straightforward love between two people who are free to love together
and express their passion as seems to them best is no good to us;
it is not the stuff of literature. He dates this development from
the Middle Ages.

In the twelfth century an adulterer or adulteress suddenly
became somebody 'interesting'. King David, in lying with
Bath-sheba, was held to have committed a crime and to have
made himself into an object of contempt. But when Tristan
carries off Iseult, his deed turns into romance, and he makes
himself into an object of admiration. What had hitherto been
a 'fault' and what could only give rise to edifying remarks on
the perils of sin and on remorse now became — in symbol —
something mystically virtuous, and later on was degraded (in
literature) into a disturbing and alluring entanglement.[6]

There is ample literary evidence of our preoccupation with
illicit passion (not only adulterous passion). What is perhaps more
interesting is the *absence* of a solid body of literature giving expression to the emotions of men and women who have enjoyed
permanent relationship — we seem, for example, to have nothing
analagous to the many Chinese poems which tenderly, and
out of an extraordinary calm and stillness, distil the love between
husband and wife, or even the love between 'the lord' and his
mistress of long standing. It is not that this kind of permanent,
profound, fulfilled relationship does not exist in the West; we may
think of the love between Rodin and his mistress Rose Beuret
which began in their twenties and ended in their seventies when
she died, or of a good, obviously satisfying marriage like that of
the Webbs; it is that it has become somehow lost as a tradition
in our literature.

De Rougemont, who takes up a somewhat aggressive
Christian stance, has firm views about what has happened. In his
opinion we have debased the myth — the myth of a happy love
between two people — and given a spurious glamour to adultery.
He makes the interesting point that *Tristan* and other adulterous
myths have many parallels to mystical writing, in particular to
the writing of St. John of the Cross and the Spanish school.

[6] Denis de Rougemont, *Passion and Society* (Faber, 1956).

The continual process of searching, finding and then losing which the saint describes as the soul's quest for God, together with the terrible suffering that this entails, are strongly reminiscent of the almost arbitrary way that Tristan and Iseult are cast together and then wrenched apart. The myth of adultery may therefore, in his view, be a kind of sick and negative version of *via mystica*.

Not surprisingly he feels this as a slight on Christianity and a bastardisation of its teaching. He does not really consider, however, whether by placing such a weighty prohibition on extra-marital sex, the Church may not have provided precisely the obstacle which gave adultery its romantic kick, and so inadvertently killed the innocent celebration of love, married or otherwise, which we find in the Chinese poems, or Gilgamesh, or *The Odyssey*, or (it is important to remember) in the Old Testament. De Rougemont, by taking the story of David and Bath-sheba out of context, has ignored the truly nauseating aspect of it which was that David, as a result of his lust, arranged for the 'accidental' death of Bath-sheba's husband.

De Rougemont regards the Tristan stories, or the adulterous elements in Arthurian legend, as a kind of playing with fire, an indulgence in sick emotions which can only lead to dissatisfaction and heartbreak. Yet I wonder if we may pick and choose between myths in this fashion, accepting the ones which express our private vision of truth, and rejecting those which seem to cast doubts upon it. If we are going to listen at all to the voice of man's unconscious then we must be humble enough to hear even the unpalatable comments, and to trust the myth to know things that we do not. If our usual attitude to myth is one of trust then we cannot too easily side with de Rougemont and decide in advance that *Tristan* is simply a portrait of man's sickness, or a debased, foolish, muddled version of St. John of the Cross. Myth, even if it describes a sick condition (as, for instance, *The Sleeping Beauty* could be said to describe neurosis), points to wholeness and the route by which it may eventually be achieved. In this sense every myth is, in my view, about *via mystica*, though some of them only attempt to describe early stages of the journey.

The Tristan legend (I am using the Beroul version here) strains at language and common sense in trying to say something real and life-giving about the human condition. It is full of contradiction and absurdity, but what I want to suggest is the most curious thing about it is the way that, without embarrassment, it can hold two opposing points of view at the same time. Point of view A, as held by Beroul, is that of a conventional Christian of his time. A couple, Tristan and Yseut, are indulging freely in the sin of adultery, wounding the pride and honour of Yseut's husband, King Mark, and flouting the wisdom and advice of Holy Church. Their love is destructive and wicked. Point of view B (held with equal firmness by Beroul), regards the couple as innocent whatever they do. This is partly because they are more sinned against than sinning (they behave as they do only because they drank a love potion not intended for them), but has more to do perhaps with their own inner conviction of their own essential innocence, no matter what they have done. Beroul can describe, with the enthusiasm of a detective, the fact that blood from a hunting wound of Tristan's has stained the Queen's bed. He can say 'Tristan slipped under the sheets without another word and held the queen in his arms'.[7] Yet at other points he seems vague about whether the couple really sleep together. Nor do they themselves seem entirely sure whether or not they commit adultery. Asked to swear their innocence they do so with a kind of passionate intensity that bewilders us, because it does not appear to be lying in any normal sense. Yseut, it is true, resorts to an element of verbal trickery in her vows. But Tristan's own declarations ring with confidence in the essential rightness of his actions. Restoring Yseut to King Mark after their sojourn in the Forest, at the behest of the hermit, he makes an unrepentant speech:

King, I hereby restore to you the noble Yseut. No man ever made a better restitution. I see the men of your land here; in their hearing I want to request you to allow me to clear myself and make my defence in your court. Never at any time did she or I love each other wickedly. You have been led to believe lies; but, as God gives me joy and happiness, they never put it to the test in a combat on foot or otherwise. If I agree to this taking place in your court, then burn me in sulphur if I am found guilty! If I can come safe through the ordeal, let no one, long-haired or bald, ever accuse us again . . .

[7] Beroul, *The Romance of Tristan*, tr. Alan S. Fedrick (Penguin, 1946).

What are we to make of this firm declaration? Whatever Tristan may say, we know that it is not lies that the king has been led to believe; in the currency of Beroul's audience Tristan and Yseut *have* loved each other 'wickedly'.

Yet it all reads less as if Tristan were a bare-faced liar than a genuinely bewildered man, who at times feels profoundly guilty and at other times perfectly innocent. Beroul himself seems every bit as confused. Those who try to warn the king in the story that he is being made a fool of are repeatedly accused of wickedness by the author, and he tells us at length of the beauty, courage, and suffering of the hero and heroine. Yet he is careful never to side completely with the lovers, nor to approve *directly* of their illicit union. The famous scene in the Forest of Morrois, in which King Mark happens upon the lovers sleeping, puts the ambiguity of the story in a nut-shell. Having caught them in what should have been the ultimately compromising posture, King Mark himself still has not got the answer to the question which torments him.

> The bower was made of green branches with foliage in places, and the ground was well covered with leaves. First Yseut lay down; then Tristan drew his sword, put it between their bodies and lay down himself. Yseut was wearing her tunic . . . and Tristan kept his trousers on . . . Hear how they were lying. She had put one arm under Tristan's neck and the other, I think, over him; her arms were clasped tightly round him. Tristan in his turn had his arms around her, for their affection was not feigned. Their mouths were closed together, yet there was a space between them and their bodies were not touching. . . .

Even King Mark is drawn into tenderness. 'God', said the king, 'what can this be? . . . I can well believe, if I have any sense that if they loved each other wickedly they would certainly not be wearing clothes, and there would be no sword between them. They would be lying together quite differently . . . They have no mind for a wicked love.'

It is not difficult to parallel the Tristan story with the story of Lancelot and Guinevere. Lancelot also loves a queen, he also makes vows to abandon the queen for a life of penitence and then quickly breaks them, he brings his love and himself to the point of ruin, and together they bring extensive suffering to themselves and others. Of the various authors who wrote of Lancelot a number reveal just the same sort of ambivalence as that shown by Beroul. Malory, in particular, manages to make it clear, though without ever directly saying it, that he believes Lancelot to be just as much on 'the worshipful way' (the vocation of all honourable men) as any of the more virtuous characters in the Arthurian tale. What gives the Lancelot material a special interest is that, unlike the Tristan story, it does not stand by itself. It is part of a wider and much more ambitious canvas, and what that describes is, of course, the quest of the Holy Grail.

The quest of the Grail is the description of a mystical journey, though equally, as psychological commentators have been quick to point out, it is full of sexual implications, the most important being that the Grail King, sitting in his castle in the middle of a devastated countryside, is gravely wounded 'in the thighs'.

> The King can only be restored to health if a knight of con-
> spicuous excellence finds the castle and at the first sight of what
> he sees there asks a certain question ... Should he finally
> succeed, after much wandering and many adventures, in find-
> ing the Grail Castle ... and should he ask the question, the
> king will be restored to health, the land will begin to grow
> green, and the hero will become the guardian of the Grail from
> that time on.[8]

The different versions of Arthurian legend offer a number of different candidates as potential guardians of the Grail, but the overwhelming favourite, at least in the early stages of the quest, is Lancelot, whose strength, courage and chastity are a by-word. At a crucial moment in the quest, however, Lancelot turns aside from the utter dedication needed for the Grail quest and devotes himself to Guinevere. There begins a painful passage in which he is alternately absorbed in his loving, and racked with remorse at breaking the laws of God and the Church. It is sharply brought home to him that he has forfeited the full access to the Grail which was to have been his, yet as R. T. Davies, the editor of Malory, points out 'such is the quality of the life he lives "in the world" that, when he leaves it to seek the Grail, he is able to achieve

8 *The Grail Legend.*

almost as much spiritually as one who has always rejected it'. The perfect, and not quite human Galahad, Lancelot's son by Elaine, inherits Lancelot's portion.

What should, I think, be of especial interest to us is the ambivalence with which stories like that of Tristan and Lancelot were told. The authors invite us to do two mutually contradictory things — to be as shocked and disapproving as their numerous hermits, ever waiting to hear a confession and suggest a painful penitence, and simultaneously to love and sympathise with these tortured lovers. We are asked to accept that they are both wicked and good; like children in a too strict home, we operate two standards — Theirs and Ours, or God's and Man's.

If we remember the way myth deals with man's deepest insights, and helps him to resolve his conflicts, then I think we must recognise here that, hundreds of years before the conflict was to break surface in social *mores*, men were struggling with new intuitions about the Christian sexual ethic. It is important to remember that the struggle took place within a quest for wholeness — the wholeness of the Grail — that it included the insight that the country in which the central action took place was devastated, and that this derived from the suffering of a King who was wounded 'in his thighs'.

What really is the conflict being described? One of the difficulties in elucidating this is that there is in my view, a double conflict, a conflict within a conflict. On the deeper level there is the conflict, indigenous to medieval Christianity, of how a man might reconcile the claims of the flesh with the claims of the spirit. But laid over this is another conflict, bearing the marks of repression, which is the conflict which came from the author's fear that what he wanted to say could not be heard by the people he wanted to say it to. He knew very well that what he had in hand was a daring operation, and that all too easily he could bring down upon his head obloquy, charges of heresy, or worse. In a society constituted as was the medieval society, no writer who hoped to survive could make the simple statement 'I think Tristan (or Lancelot) may have been engaged on *via mystica*.' He could only hint at the possibility, draw attention to it by being shocked at it and protect his hero by making careful obeisances in the direction of all the sacred cows.

Yet nevertheless these voices emerge with a touching clarity saying, not that 'adultery is all right', but that man's quest for wholeness is essentially a mysterious business, that it has its own vocation which may lead some to disgrace and the terrible responsibility of wounding others as surely as it leads others into more obvious forms of selflessness. And perhaps above all that a man, or a people, or a Church, or the human race, cannot leave sexuality on one side in the journey towards wholeness without 'devastating the countryside'. Tristan and Lancelot who, with the exception of Oedipus, are the most tortured human beings in the history of myth, are, to my mind, also the bravest. It is the task of heroes to blaze out new trails, to think the unthinkable, to extend the tiny clearing of consciousness and responsibility into the vast forest of blindness and darkness. Each of these two takes on the collective and its crude judgment in hopeless contest, and is crucified upon its fear and hatred.

Yet it must also be said that all the major myths carry a motif of suffering. For Tristan and Lancelot it is the central theme of their lives; for Gilgamesh, Odysseus, Beowulf, the suffering lies in the anguish of their pride and strength being confronted by the brute forces of nature, and in particular the force of mortality. What we are forced to watch is the humbling of giants.

Gilgamesh is broken by his terrible journey, when he at last confronts Utnapishtim, 'the Faraway'. 'I have wandered over the world, I have crossed many difficult ranges, I have crossed the sea, I have wearied myself with travelling; my joints are aching, and I have lost acquaintance with sleep which is sweet.' Finally, almost unexpectedly, he wrests from Utnapishtim the secret he longs for. 'There is a plant', he is told, 'that grows under the water, it has a prickle like a thorn, like a rose; it will wound your hands, but if you succeed in taking it, then your hands will hold that which restores his lost youth to a man.'

Gilgamesh plucks this wonderful plant and begins to travel back to Uruk where he will 'give it to the old men to eat'. On the way he pauses to bathe in a well of cool water where, unbeknown to him, a serpent is hidden. It rises out of the water and snatches his precious flower away from him. 'Then Gilgamesh sat down and wept, the tears ran down his face, and he took the hand of Urshanabi; "O Urshanabi, was it for this that I toiled with my hands, is it for this I have wrung out my heart's blood? For myself I have gained nothing . . . I found a sign and now I have lost it." '

Beowulf also dies in despair. Always supremely strong, the aged king has a premonition as he goes to confront his last monster. He stands upon a headland and broods upon the task before him.

His mind was uneasy and restless, anticipating the end. The doom which was to attend the old hero, probe the resources of his soul, and tear the life from his body, was close at hand. Not much longer would flesh enclose the spirit of the king . . . It was no easy thing for Beowulf to make up his mind to quit this world and take up his lodging in some other, whether he liked it or not. But this is the way in which everyone has to die.

Burning in the flames of the fiery dragon, and unable to wound the creature with his sword, Beowulf has to accept the help of a young prince. It is the young man who decisively wounds the creature, whereas Beowulf is mortally hurt. Before he dies he bestows his golden helmet, corselet and ring to the young hero who will inherit his fame.

The journey of Odysseus, though it carries suffering enough, comes to a happier conclusion, or rather two conclusions. The ultimate conclusion lies in Odysseus once again assuming his throne and casting out the upstart suitors, but the first, and more moving, conclusion lies in the hero's return to his own longed-for country. The friendly Phaeacians set the sleeping man down upon the shore, pile his treasures near him, and quietly leave him. When he wakes he does not at first grasp the truth — that all his terrible suffering has at last led him home, and that he is ready once more to assume the throne which his enemies had supposed he had abdicated. 'The end of all our exploring', says Eliot,

> Will be to arrive where we started
> And know the place for the first time.

It is interesting to compare these descriptions with the ending of the journey of the overtly Christian Lancelot. The twelfth-century *Quest of the Holy Grail*, part of the huge French version known as 'the Lancelot cycle' is the one which most surely captures the spiritual meaning of Lancelot's adventures. What it describes, as it comes to the climax of the story, is a man steadily stripping away, or being stripped of, the pride, the little conceits, the vanities, the lusts, which have kept him going, and moving inexorably into a situation where there is no room left to manoeuvre. It *could* be read as an allegory for the humiliation of old age. Or it could be read as a description of an experience deeply engrained in the human situation, but one which Christianity pre-eminently has talked about and tried to understand. I mean the experience of death-within-life. For life to go on, it must contain death — the seed must lie dormant in the ground and eventually rot for the shoot to come forth. In human terms this involves a sudden or gradual increase of mental pain which goes on increasing to the point where it becomes intolerable. The subject looks frantically for a path of escape, but all roads seem mysteriously closed to him; nevertheless, in his desperation, he continues to believe that there *must* be a way out. Yet the violence of his struggles only aggravates his suffering. Finally, he submits in a gesture of dignity and complexity. He surrenders, yet there is nothing degrading about it; it is a proper submission to the inevitable process of life. He is in despair — it is this which constitutes his agony — yet within the despair he experiences an inexplicable hope.

Lancelot comes to his crucifixion and resurrection (the words which Christianity uses to describe the process of transformation) when all that he has valued has been taken from him. He has endured the unfamiliar experience of defeat in battle, he has given up Guinevere, he is consumed with sorrow at having lost his way on the Grail journey, and he is weak from the many acts of penitence and mourning that this loss has forced upon him. He is utterly lonely, and he prays continually and with a desperate intensity. Finally, his horse, the last symbol of knightly pride and his only hope in escaping from the desolate country in which he finds himself, is killed under him by a black knight who mysteriously appears 'out of the river' for this purpose.

Thus was Lancelot hemmed in on all sides: in front flowed the river, to either side rose the cliffs, and at his back lay the forest. With whatever attention he considered these obstacles, he could see no salvation here below. For if he clambered up the cliffs and needed to eat he would find nothing to satisfy his hunger, unless Our Lord saw to it. And if he entered the forest, which was more treacherous than any he had known he could lose his way and wander many days without finding a soul to help him. And as for the river, he did not see how he could make the crossing safely, for the water was so deep and dark that he would have no footing.[9]

Lancelot realises that there is nothing to be done but to stay where he is. 'When darkness was fast mingling with the ebbing day, Lancelot took off his armour, and lying down beside it commended himself to God ... His prayer ended, he fell asleep. ...'

In his sleep he dreams that he is being told to get up and step upon a boat which he will find on the river. In a state between waking and sleeping he climbs into the boat, thanking Christ as he does so. 'Thereupon he propped himself against the side of the boat and fell asleep in this beatitude. Lancelot passed that night in a state of such tranquillity and bliss that he fancied he was not his wonted self, but a man transformed.' The boat is to take him, first, to a tender reunion with his son Galahad, and finally to the castle where he has his partial vision of the Holy Grail.

This realisation of the creative and redemptive aspects of suffering lies at the heart of Christianity, but in so far as all religious truths are universal truths it is implicit in a writer like Sophocles who is deeply immersed in the problem of suffering, or a writer like Apuleius who had scant sympathy for the Christians. There is, in my view, no more terrible evocation of human suffering than the two Oedipus plays. The suffering of Oedipus is that of a man who has realised that torment lies not in external events but within himself, and who tries, vainly, to rescue himself by the desperate remedy of blindness. 'The physical agony of Oedipus', writes E. F. Watling,' is but the counterpart to the spiritual torture of self-knowledge. Or as the other blind man of the play, Teiresias, remarks,

O, when wisdom brings no profit,
To be wise is to suffer.

9 *The Quest of the Holy Grail*, tr. P. M. Matarasso (Penguin, 1969).

Yet, as Sophocles recognises in *Oedipus at Colonus* suffering has changed and cleansed and transformed Oedipus till he is almost unrecognisable as the brash young ruler at the beginning of *Oedipus Rex*. 'My strength has been in suffering' says Oedipus, and again 'Three masters — pain, time and the royalty in the blood — have taught me patience.' In his old age Oedipus arrives at a sacred country which he recognises as the place where he should end his days. He is summoned by a god whose voice terrified all who heard it. 'Oedipus! Oedipus!' it cried, again and again. 'It is time: you stay too long.' Mysteriously, gloriously, Oedipus is taken by the gods, watched only by King Theseus.

But the King was standing alone holding his hand before his eyes as if he had seen some terrible sight that no one could bear to look upon . . . In what manner Oedipus passed from this earth, no one can tell. Only Theseus knows. We know he was not destroyed by a thunderbolt from heaven nor tide-wave rising from the sea, for no such thing occurred. Maybe a guiding spirit from the gods took him, or the earth's foundations gently opened and received him with no pain. Certain it is that he was taken without a pang, without grief or agony — a passing more wonderful than that of any other man. What I have said will seem, perhaps, like some wild dream of fancy, beyond belief. If so, then you must disbelieve it. I can say no more.[10]

[10] Sophocles, *Oedipus at Colonus*, tr. E. F. Watling (Penguin, 1947).

CHAPTER FOUR

Journey of Faith

ALL ATTEMPTS AT DESCRIBING JOURNEY ARE RELIGIOUS, in that they are concerned with meaning, with the attempt to 'gather together' relevant material about what it is to be a human being, or how to be a human being. All move into mystery. This is as true in the case of homely fairy tales with their buried sexual implications as in the solemnities of the Grail story, with its talk of God and Christ and the Christian virtues (and *its* buried sexual implications). In the landscape of myth everything is religious.

It is only as consciousness grows that man begins to notice he is religious, or feels the need to remind himself to be so. Folktales do not have the need to refer to God with the insistence they do in the Grail stories, simply because the writers take God as totally for granted as the air they breathe. There is always a heavy price to be paid for consciousness, and the price we have paid in this instance is 'religion' or 'faith', a much more cerebral attempt to hold on to numinous insights. Something natural and carefree has been lost; something disciplined has been found.

Christianity developed the theme of journey, making the search for God explicit, and tending either to play down the sexual element in it all, or else disguising its sexuality from itself by such devices as Mariolatry or by dwelling on themes, such as the crucifixion, which allow of a sado-masochistic content. One thinks of many paintings of the German school, or of literature like the beautiful '*Quia amore langueo*', in which Christ addresses the soul:

My fair love and my spouse bright!
I saved her from beating, and she hath me bet;
I clothed her in grace and heavenly light;
This bloody shirt hath on me set;
For longing of love yet would I not let;
Sweet strokes are these: lo!
I have loved her as I het
    Quia amore langueo.

Yet apart from its difficulty in integrating the sexual aspects of man (an obviously important task in the finding of meaning), Christianity did produce some magnificent literature on the theme of journey. Christian journeys represent a sort of half-way house between the artlessness of myth and modern disillusion. Christianity represents a growth in consciousness. The Christian writers know what the earlier writers and story tellers did not consciously know — that journeys are about meaning and about God. What on the other hand the Christian writers do not know consciously is that God and meaning are inextricably bound up with sexuality. It is this later insight which we have found so hard to integrate into our understanding of meaning, some preferring to abandon any attempt at faith rather than strive to do so, others seeking to bury their heads in Puritan sand rather than wrestle with the problems involved.

The very vehemence with which sexuality is denied makes it shout aloud in Christian writers about journey. Bunyan's ceaseless battle with anxiety and depressive doubts and fears, and St. John of the Cross's sexual imagery as he describes the soul moving towards *unio mystica*, reveal the strength and dominance of the instinctual life when it is denied. The Fisher King was indeed wounded in his thighs.

There are, roughly speaking, two sets of Christian journeys. One set is steeped in an active approach to the world, and is about the struggle of men to live out an inner truth in an uncomprehending and often cruel world. The other set has been about the contemplative and mystical approach as the soul is led along a path that takes it towards union with God — a deeply introverted journey which is the way of those who discover, like the Chinese Lao Tzu, that 'without looking out of the window you can see the way of Heaven'.

In general the Evangelical tradition has been the most thorough in exploring the active route, and describing the journey, Bunyan being the greatest exponent, followed by Law, the Wesleys, Kingsley and others. Even *Tom Brown's Schooldays* and a book like *Little Women* are caught up in this drama of the Christian in the world, ever ready to proclaim the truth that is in him at the cost of having shoes thrown at him in the dormitory when he says his prayers, or having to endure the scorn of the rich and worldly at his simple and chaste ways. Huge tracts of Victorian literature, particularly those intended for children, were influenced by this kind of Christianity, and were persuaded by it that simplicity of life, honesty, chastity, obedience to parents and betters, sobriety, charity were the marks that the Christian journey was being undertaken. The family in *Little Women* never touch alcohol except when ill, and give away their breakfast to a poor family on Christmas Day.

It is, of course, a far cry from the blazing genius of Bunyan to the sentimentality of Victorian children's books. Whereas the Victorian writers (with honourable exceptions like Kingsley) tend to be much more interested in charity than in attacking the appalling social conditions which made it necessary, Bunyan was a political firebrand, who spent twelve years, on and off, in prison for refusing to 'conform' to the Church of England. What perhaps the later generations of writers took from him most surely, and it has buried itself deeply in the whole Evangelical tradition of Christianity, is paranoia, the sense of one's own rightness and other people's persecutory wrongness, a theme which recurs almost constantly throughout *Pilgrim's Progress*. The others, in Bunyan's case 'the world', are seen as persecutory, a threat to one's very existence, so that it becomes a pressing matter to convert them.

Bunyan regarded the whole Christian journey as 'desperate'. He thought it desperate, partly because it seemed to him that if a man tried to ally himself with the truth then inevitably he incurred the hatred of the world; certainly there was much in Bunyan's own life to confirm such a view. And he believed it desperate in a second sense because this world, with all its beauties and distractions, is ultimately perishable. The only way to 'have life' is to set one's desire on something beyond it, and rely on the strength of this desire to take you safely, despite sins

and errors, past all the demons and disasters which await a man
on his journey to the grave. Christian in *Pilgrim's Progress* sets
out from the City of Destruction because he is afraid of being
destroyed by fire. He endures the terrible labours and the heartrending fears of the journey because he wants to get to the
Celestial City and he knows that none of the joys of the wayside
are of lasting good to him. His word for salvation is 'Life', and
desperately shouting 'Life, life, eternal life' he sets off running
from the City of Destruction, his fingers stuffed in his ears to
prevent him hearing the cries of his relatives and neighbours.

It is striking that there are many fewer images of God's love in
Pilgrim's Progress than there are images of fear, despair, anxiety,
and damnation. Bunyan's autobiography shows that Bunyan
suffered all his life from severe depression, an acute sense of guilt,
and even at times demonic hallucination. His own suffering is
poignantly revealed on almost every page of the *Progress*, and it
is not difficult to guess the identity of the man in the iron cage.

Man: I am now a man of despair, and am shut up in it, as in
this iron cage. I cannot get out, O now I cannot . . .

Christian: Then said Christian, Is there no hope but you must
be kept in this iron cage of despair?

Man: No, none at all.

Christian: Why? The Son of the Blessed is very pitiful.

Man: (Giving long list of his sins). God hath denied me repentance; his word gives me no encouragement to believe; yea,
himself hath shut me up in this iron cage: nor can all the
men in the world let me out. O eternity! eternity! how
shall I grapple with the misery that I must meet with in
eternity?[1]

The Pilgrim's Progress is Bunyan's attempt to show how Man
is helped out of his prison. There are passages of great tenderness
and peace as the heroes of the book — Christian, Christiana,
Faithful, Mr. Great-Heart, Mr. Valiant-for-Truth — begin to
perceive the goal towards which they have been half-blindly
striving.

[1] John Bunyan, *The Pilgrim's Progress*, ed. Roger Sharrock (Penguin,
1965).

The Pilgrims said 'Whose goodly vineyards and gardens are these?' He (the gardener) answered 'They are the King's, and are planted here for his own delights, and also for the solace of pilgrims.' So the gardener had them into the vineyards, and bid them refresh themselves with the dainties; he also showed them there the King's walks and the arbours where he delighted to be ...

The reflection of the sun upon the City was so extremely glorious that they could not, as yet, with open face behold it ... but through an instrument made for that purpose ...

The thoughts of what I am going to, and of the conduct that waits for me on the other side, doth lie as a glowing coal at my heart. I see myself now at the end of my journey, my toilsome days are ended. I am going now to see that head that was crowned with thorns, and that face that was spit upon, for me. I have formerly lived by hear-say and faith, but now I go where I shall live by sight, and shall be with him, in whose company I delight myself.

Bunyan is here allying himself with a very strong, though not universal, Christian tradition, which placed joy and the satis- faction of desire in a future state. Christian and Hopeful fall ill with desire when they catch a glimpse of the golden towers of the City in the distance, and this symbolises the way generations of Christians, both Catholic and Protestant, saw the Christian journey — a desire which conflicted with, and involved the extinction of, the desires of this world. In this life we could expect no more than the occasional tantalising glimpse of glory, and it was a glory which inevitably insisted upon sacrifice.

Modern theology looks with a good deal of embarrassment at this ancient Christian emphasis and insists on the incarnational nature of Christianity, claiming that the Kingdom is now and here, not in some other dimension of time and space, yet there is something gripping and true about Bunyan's reminder that men in agony, spiritual, physical, psychological, are in hell, or near to it. Christian, blindly seeking the Celestial City, in agony, physical distress, and blind fear, is a heartrending figure. His God, though basically loving, is stern, and curiously unreasonable, a father who insists on hiding from a terrified child, and who thinks that the way to bring him up is to force him, confused and

alarmed, over a lethal obstacle course. This may not be the God
of the New Testament; it is the God whom many Christians,
depressed and guilt-ridden, made in the image of their own
experience.

Bunyan's bleak Calvinism and the mental agony that it produced evokes R. S. Thomas:

> Protestantism — the adroit castrator
> Of art; the bitter negation
> Of song and dance and the heart's innocent joy —
> You have botched our flesh and left us only the soul's
> Terrible impotence in a warm world.

But Catholicism too has claimed its own plentiful victims of a
cramped vision.

There is, perhaps, a sense in which Christian's journey has a
more uniquely Protestant flavour. It is in the utter loneliness of
the figure of Christian, a man of heightened self-awareness, a
kind of Prometheus. The contradictions and absurdities of
Catholicism which left the senses room to manoeuvre, along with
the sense of being deep-rooted at an unconscious level in a rich
and satisfying soil, are denied to this poor pilgrim.

But tragic as Christian is, he is not pathetic, and though his
descendants may have shown the marks of spiritual castration,
as Bunyan writes about him he is a virile figure, who brings a
tremendous and orgasmic passion to everything he attempts.

His great asset is his over-riding sense of purpose, a purpose
which runs through every sentence Bunyan writes, and becomes,
at the end of the first part of *Pilgrim's Progress*, and even more
at the end of the second part, an exploding rocket of joy. Life is
deeply, almost unbearably, meaningful.

His sense of meaning is what gives Bunyan's pilgrim his extraordinary poise in the face of every sort of discouragement, the
discouragement of his relatives who thought 'that some frenzy
distemper had got into his head' and the ridicule of the inhabit-
ants of Vanity Fair. 'Some said they were fools, some they were
bedlams, and some "They are outlandish-men".'

Christian and Faithful, under examination, say straightfor-
wardly that they are 'pilgrims and strangers in the world, and
that they were going to their own country, which was the heavenly

Jerusalem' and they bring down the wrath of the mob upon themselves. They are subjected to cruel ill-treatment and public humiliation, and Faithful is eventually 'put to the most cruel death that could be invented'.

Christian's sense of inner purpose not only gives him poise in enduring the miseries which 'the world' inflicts on him, but also helps him to stand outside the follies and brutalities of the mob, and view them in perspective. The poise is, of course, Bunyan's. He has taken the measure of Mr. Worldly Wiseman who 'favoureth only the doctrine of his world (therefore he always goes to the town of Morality to church)' and who 'loveth that doctrine best, for it saveth him from the Cross'.

Bunyan notes that in 'the world' everything is for sale

as houses, lands, trades, places, honours, preferments, titles, countries, kingdoms, lusts, pleasures, and delights of all sorts, as whores, bawds, wives, husbands, children, masters, servants, lives, blood, bodies, souls, silver, gold, pearls, precious stones, and what not . . .

Here are to be seen too, and that for nothing, thefts, murders, adulteries, false-swearers, and that of a blood-red colour.

Bunyan would rather be persecuted by such a world than collude with it.

One of the most moving aspects of Bunyan's pilgrim is his profound experience of psychological suffering. While it may seem to us that Puritanism encouraged morbidity by its enormous emphasis on guilt and hell-fire, it does at least take men's suffering with the utmost seriousness, it grants them the dignity of it, and offers a way of dealing with it. A man was allowed, and expected, to experience despair, fear, gloom, loneliness, and horror, without any of our twentieth-century indignation at such pains, or belief that they could be anaesthetised away by pills or better welfare.

Christian has scarcely set off before he plunges up to his eyebrows in the Slough of Despond, but far worse things are to follow. On the Hill Difficulty, hard by the way to Destruction, Christian tries to escape his sorrows in sleep, and therefore has to make a journey in the dark that he might have made by daylight. 'I must walk without the sun, darkness must cover the path of my feet, and I must hear the noise of doleful creatures, because of my sinful sleep.'

Surviving the Valley of Humiliation where he fights with Apollyon, the Prince of this World, Christian finds himself in the Valley of the Shadow of Death, 'a very solitary place'. He is warned by some other wayfarers of what lies ahead.

'What have you seen?' said Christian.

Men: Seen! Why the Valley itself, which is as dark as pitch; we also saw there the hobgoblins, satyrs, and dragons of the pit: we heard also in that Valley a continual howling and yelling, as of a people under unutterable misery who there sat bound in affliction and irons: and over that Valley hangs the discouraging clouds of confusion; death also doth always spread his wings over it: in a word, it is every whit dreadful, being utterly without order.

In the Valley the pilgrim has to tread a delicate path between the ditch, into which the blind lead the blind, and 'a very dangerous quag, into which, if even a good man falls he can find no bottom for his foot to stand on.' Treading this terrifying path alone, Christian suddenly finds himself looking down into the mouth of Hell itself.

Yet even now his mental sufferings are not yet complete. In Doubting Castle, maltreated by Giant Despair, Christian and Hopeful reach the lowest point. 'When he came there he found them alive, and truly, alive was all: for now, what for want of bread and water, and by reason of the wounds they received when he beat them, they could do little but breathe.' They are tormented by a longing to commit suicide.

Christian's final agony comes upon him as he goes down into the River of Death which he must cross in order to reach the Celestial City.

A great darkness and horror fell upon Christian, so that he could not see before him; also he here in great measure lost his senses, so that he could neither remember nor orderly talk of any of those sweet refreshments that he had met with in the way of his pilgrimage. . . . He had horror of mind and hearty fears that he should die in that River, and never obtain entrance in at the Gate ... 'Twas also observed that he was troubled with apparitions of hobgoblins and evil spirits ...

But there are comforts for each of Christian's bouts of suffering. Early in his pilgrimage he discovers that the great weight of guilt which he carries on his shoulders is loosed and tumbles off when he sees the Cross. This arouses in him the deepest emotions of grief and joy. 'He looked therefore, and looked again, even till the springs that were in his head sent the waters down his cheeks.'

After the Hill Difficulty comes the House Beautiful, after the 'solitary way' through the Valley of the Shadow he is befriended by Faithful, having discovered something he calls All-Prayer, which is a kind of surrendering oneself to God's providence. After the horrors of Doubting Castle, from which he and Hopeful are delivered with a key called Promise, they are refreshed in the vineyards of the Delectable Mountains. Finally, after the last terrifying passage through the River, they enter in at the Gate of the Celestial City and 'lo, as they entered they were transfigured, and they had raiment put on that shone like gold. ... All the bells in the City rang again for joy; and it was said unto them "Enter ye into the joy of your Lord." ' Christ, the pilgrims had been told early in their journey, 'had made many pilgrims princes, though by nature they were beggars born, and their original had been the dunghill'.

Roger Sharrock, Bunyan's editor, suggests that the imagination of Bunyan and other Puritan Englishmen had been nourished on a rich religious soil. 'Life was a confrontation between the powers of light and the powers of darkness, or, to change the metaphor, the adventurous journey of the armed and vigilant Christian through hostile country.' And he quotes a pamphlet about the Puritan by a contemporary, John Geree: 'His whole life he accounted a warfare wherein Christ was his Captaine, his armes, prayers and teares, the Crosse his Banner ...'

The map of the journey is briefly, but adequately sketched out by Mr. Great-Heart and Mr. Valiant-for-Truth.

Great-Heart: Was your father and mother willing that you should become a pilgrim?
Valiant-for-Truth: Oh, no. They used all means imaginable to persuade me to stay at home.

Great-Heart: Why, what could they say against it?

Valiant-for-Truth: They said it was an idle life, and if I myself were not inclined to sloth and laziness, I would never countenance a pilgrim's condition.

Great-Heart: And what did they say else?

Valiant-for-Truth: Why, they told me that it was a dangerous way, yea the most dangerous way in the world, said they, is that which the pilgrims go.

Great-Heart: Did they show wherein this way is so dangerous?

Valiant-for-Truth: Yes, and that in many particulars.

Great-Heart: Name some of them.

Valiant-for-Truth: They told me of the Slough of Despond where Christian was well nigh smothered. They told me that there were archers standing ready in Beelzebub-Castle, to shoot them that should knock at the Wicket Gate for entrance. They told me also of the wood, and dark mountains, of the Hill Difficulty, of the lions, and also of the three giants, Bloodyman, Maul, and Slay-good. They said moreover, that there was a foul fiend haunted the Valley of Humiliation, and that Christian was, by him, almost bereft of life. 'Besides' said they, 'you must go over the Valley of the Shadow of Death, where the hobgoblins are, where the light is darkness, where the way is full of snares, pits, traps and gins.' They told me also of Giant Despair, of Doubting Castle, and of the ruins that the pilgrims met with there. Further, they said I must go over the Enchanted Ground, which was dangerous. And that after all this I should find a River over which I should find no bridge, and that that River did lie betwixt me and the Celestial City . . .

Great-Heart: I promise you, this was enough to discourage. But did they make an end here?

Valiant-for-Truth: No, stay. They told me also of many that had tried that way of old, and that had gone a great way therein, to see if they could find something of the glory there that so many had so much talked of from time to time, and how they came back again, and befooled themselves for setting a foot out of doors in that path . . .

Great-Heart: And did none of these things discourage you?

Valiant-for-Truth: No. They seemed but as so many nothings to me.

Great-Heart: How came that about?

Valiant-for-Truth: Why, I still believed what Mr. Tell-true had said, and that carried me beyond them all.

Great-Heart: Then this was your victory, even your faith?

Valiant-for-Truth: It was so, I believed and therefore came out, got into the way, fought all that set themselves against me, and by believing am come to this place.

The Calvinist dramatisation of the human lot perhaps came more easily to men who were suffering hardship and persecution. But some of the same sort of suffering, though expressed in more refined and luxurious imagery, appears in the poetry of George Herbert, another great Christian voice of the seventeenth century. Herbert had none of Bunyan's social or cultural disadvantages. He was the son, not of a tinker, but of aristocratic stock, he had a good education and considerable hopes of a diplomatic career, and he was an Anglican. Yet, after a disappointment at Court and a serious illness, he decided to take Holy Orders, and became a country parish priest. He is less paranoid about the world than Bunyan, but the awareness of its triviality, its heartless frivolity, and its domination of the senses, has bitten deeply into his poetry. The world is a world of 'sugred lies', yet at times he pines for all that he has given up. He experiences, and describes, the intense frustration which his changed life at times imposes upon him, yet he believes that the kind of freedom he is seeking, the freedom of God's love, must be sought in solitude and simplicity.

Yet he knows himself a man racked by contradictions, not the contradictions of Bunyan's doubt, but the pain of being a man whose vision of truth often warred with his senses — in short, the pain of being human. The Cross of Christ becomes for him the symbol of the torturing opposites within himself.

> Ah my deare Father, ease my smart!
> The contrarieties crush me: these crosse actions
> Doe winde a rope about, and cut my heart:
>   And yet since these thy contradictions
> Are properly a crosse felt by thy sonne,
> With but foure words, my words, Thy will be done.

In one poem, 'The Pilgrimage', Herbert attempts to draw the whole map of his journey. His suffering is in some ways reminiscent of Bunyan's, but as an ex-courtier and lover, his sense of loss takes a different form from that of Bunyan, the tinker who once said that he always felt shy in the company of women. The dominant theme in Herbert's poetry is the pain of what he has renounced, and whereas Bunyan sees nothing but joy when his miserable sentence on earth has finished, Herbert cannot easily see beyond the self-renunciation that progress in the love of God demands.

> I travell'd on, seeing the hill, where lay
> My expectation.
> A long it was and weary way
> The gloomy cave of Desperation.
> I left on th'one, and on the other side
> The rock of Pride . . .

The poet travels through the field of fancy, past care, and into the 'wilde of passion'. At last he reaches the hill which has been his goal through the whole painful journey and climbing up it he throws himself exhausted upon the ground. But to his horror all there is to discover is a 'lake of brackish waters', that is of tears. He is overcome with despair until he realises that there is another hill beyond the one he has found.

> My hill was further: so I flung away,
> Yet heard a crie
> Just as I went, None goes that way
> And lives: If that be all, said I,
> After so foul a journey death is fair,
> And but a chair.

After the strenuous note of Bunyan's and Herbert's journeys, it is a surprise to find oneself among the mystics who, for all their asceticism, suggest that the Christian journey lies in passivity, an inner letting go. Striving, for the mystic, is not the way to the peace he longs for. He is a man in love with God, and rather like the human lover, he grows in love by trying to be with his love, by contemplating it, by trying to achieve the inner clarity and stillness which makes it possible to feed upon his rich inner experience to the full.

A dominant theme in Christian mystical writing is that the soul is found, chosen, by God, and the Song of Solomon is again and again used to express the dance of the lovers, with its strange dreamlike figures of searching and loss, interspersed with moments of rapturous meeting. The soul, feminine to the divine lover, is consumed with passion. All the more common satisfactions become meaningless. What is longed for is a mystery which the lover can scarcely put into words.

> He that is growing to full growth
> In the desire of God profound,
> Will find his tastes so changed around
> That of mere pleasures he is loth,
> Like one who, with the fever hot,
> At food will only look askance
> But craves for that, he knows not what,
> Which may be brought by lucky chance.[2]

In his cycle of poems St. John of the Cross describes the encounters between 'the soul and the bridegroom'. The soul is plucked forth from the safety of its 'house' and moves in darkness towards its meeting with the beloved, led only by its inner longing. 'With no other light, Except for that which in my heart was burning.' Compelled upon this course, the soul, almost carelessly, forgets about all the things that once seemed important.

> So now if from this day
> I am not found among the haunts of men,
> Say that I went astray
> Love-stricken from my way.

The soul scarcely knows whether it is in a state of joy or pain. At times, because love contains parting as well as union, it is torn and wounded beyond endurance. At times, because the joy itself is so extreme, the soul is in a kind of agony of being; the quality of the emotional experience nearly shatters the fragile

[2] Poems of St. John of the Cross, tr. Roy Campbell (Penguin, 1966).

instrument with its vibration. The soul learns the magnificent strangeness of the lover.

> My Love's the mountain range,
> The Valleys each with solitary grove,
> The islands far and strange,
> The streams with sounds that change

and 'in solitude' the two lovers travel towards the climactic moment of love.

In fearless simplicity, St. John pursues his image of the soul as a virgin being ravished by God, to its proper conclusion.

> Oh flame of love so living,
> How tenderly you force
> To my soul's inmost core your fiery probe!
> Since now you've no misgiving,
> End it, pursue your course
> And for our sweet encounter tear the robe!

The soul moves into the peace which follows joy, the peace in which the boundaries of identity melt, and time melts into eternity.

> The man who truly there has come
> Of his own self must shed the guise;
> Of all he knew before the sum
> Seems far beneath that wondrous prize . . .

> If you would ask, what is its essence —
> This summit of all sense and knowing:
> It comes from the Divinest Presence —
> The sudden sense of Him outflowing,
> In His great clemency bestowing
> The gift that leaves men knowing naught,
> Yet passing knowledge with their thought.

St. John is much more explicit than many mystical writers about the femininity of the soul before God as it waits passively to receive God's gift of himself.

6—TEOOE * *

Julian of Norwich, by contrast, writes of herself rather as a child with Christ as its mother. The soul is gently taken to the breast and invited to feast upon the love and tenderness it finds there. Only the most deep and intimate expressions of tenderness seem adequate to convey the profundity of what happens between the mystic and God, and even then, as both these saints see and say, language is grossly inadequate for their purpose, and may be totally misleading.

It is this knowledge that God is not to be caught in words, and that the journey is unutterable that formed the idea which Western Christianity has called '*via negativa*'; Eastern Christianity, with the stronger tradition of it, calls it the 'apophatic' way. In both East and West Pseudo-Dionysius helped to crystallise men's thought about the negative way, though his influence established itself in Eastern Christianity centuries before it did so in the West. At the heart of his thought was the belief that God is unknowable. God so far surpasses the intellect and the senses of a man that upon encounter with God our capacity to experience breaks down. Not only is the man who experiences God caught up in a situation which is physically and mentally beyond him, but when the moment of encounter is over he has no words which can do justice to what he has experienced. Helplessly he falls back upon the words which, for human beings, evoke their most sublime moments. He turns to metaphors of kingliness, transmitting a notion of God in his glory, might, majesty, dominion and power. Or, like St. John and Julian of Norwich, he turns to the most profound human experiences of love and tenderness, and the transcending of the self which this can produce.

Yet in the end language fails him. In the end God is not 'like' a king, or 'like' a lover, or 'like' a mother with her child, but is an essence of which these metaphors and experiences are, at best, pale reflections. The mystic is always aware that he is telling a kind of lie when he uses language in this way, a lie to which he is driven by the most cruel necessity of needing to utter the unutterable. He feels obliged to warn his readers about the falsification involved.

The writers of *via negativa* however, take this compulsion much further. They begin by telling us that God is unknowable and that by the ordinary use of our intellect and our senses we cannot hope to approach him. The only way in which we can be 'oned' with God is by love and even this is not love as it is usually understood among men. It involves a setting aside of the imagery and emotion about God which may mislead us, and then a waiting in the emptiness, simplicity, bareness and darkness, which this leaves behind. 'Look that nothing live in thy working mind but a naked intent stretching into God' says the author of the *Epistle of Privy Counsel*. Dionysius, and his innumerable imitators, saw the Christian soul as setting out upon the threefold way of purgation, illumination, and (for the privileged and the brave) union. Upon this journey the soul would have many adventures, as it was overtaken by joy and by suffering. But it always remained, in a sense, in the same position, in a state of blindness and helplessness. 'Try to penetrate that darkness above you. Strike that thick cloud of unknowing with the sharp dart of longing love, and on no account whatever think of giving up.' Why must God be sought in this way, ignoring the riches of our intellects and our senses? Because God 'may well be loved, but not thought. By love he can be caught and held, but by thinking never.'[3]

Like most of the mystics, the author of the *Cloud of Unknowing* is acutely aware of the soul as playing a passive role towards God, and to the process which the journeying Christian finds unfolding within him.

> Let this deal with you and lead you as it will ... Watch it if you like, but let it alone. Do not interfere with it, as though you would help, but fear that you would spoil it all. Be the tree: let it be the carpenter. Be the house, and let it be the householder who lives there. Be willing to be blind, and give up all longing to know the why and how ...

Yet despite the helplessness and passivity of *via negativa*, it really is a way and there are landmarks for those who follow it. To begin with the soul makes the discovery that it is drawn to this kind of passivity. It feels itself called to what the Cloud calls the 'Solitary' way of life; if it were not called it would be wrong for it to undertake it. It knows too, that this is a response to the loving action of God and that its whole future life must be seen

---

[3] *The Cloud of Unknowing*, ed. Clifton Wolters (Penguin, 1970).

in terms of response to this action. 'Your whole life must now be one of longing. . . . And this longing must be in the depths of your will, put there by God, with your consent.' The soul enters into darkness, the 'Cloud of Unknowing'. 'By "darkness" I mean "a lack of knowing" — just as anything that you do not know or may have forgotten may be said to be "dark" to you, for you cannot see it with your inward eye. For this reason it is called "a cloud", not of the sky, of course, but "of unknowing", a cloud of unknowing between you and your God.'

The soul must not only endure living in this state of 'unknowing', but it must also practise detachment towards the whole created world, putting a 'cloud of forgetting' between itself and everything which helps it to forget the naked exigency of its longing for God. Stripped of its diversions and its substitutes, it settles to the task of trying to perceive God in the darkness.

The author of the *Cloud* does not pretend that this is the path for everyone. Within the Christian life there are many paths, and there are the two main divisions of Active and Contemplative. The Active Christian is called to a life busy with works of love in the world, and to penitence, worship, and meditative prayer. The Contemplative has to give himself to something apparently more nebulous. He finds himself reduced, at least in the advanced stages of his journey, to a total simplicity in which he 'is wholly caught up in darkness . . . with an outreaching love and a blind groping for the naked being of God, himself and him only.'

These two kinds of life, Active and Contemplative, lead the soul in different directions. The Cloud sees the soul as moving outwards from itself in the Active life; then, if it turns from this towards a more contemplative way of life, moving inwards; and, finally, as it learns the lessons of the contemplative life, it may move upwards into God. 'His deliberate intention is to win by grace what he cannot attain by nature, namely, to be united to God in spirit, one with him in love and will.'

The contemplative soul is forbidden to people its emptiness with imaginary companions which comfort it for its loneliness. Still less may it indulge in sentimental thoughts and feelings about God. The darkness and the emptiness must be experienced as such until they too blaze with the glory and the love of God.

The *Cloud* describes other landmarks on this mystical journey. Like Bunyan's Pilgrim the contemplative will have to endure the discouragement of his friends and relatives who will assure him that it is a very unwise undertaking in which he is bound to fail. But, alongside the pain of being misunderstood by those whom he loves, he will find, without any special labour on his part, a new love for his fellow-man welling up within him. 'All men alike are his brothers, and none strangers. He considers all men his friends, and none his foes. To such an extent that even those who hurt and injure him he reckons to be real and special friends.'

Struggling with his vision of love he becomes aware of sin, aware of it not so much in details as in a great lump that he cannot get rid of. The Cloud speaks of it almost as a cancer, a wrongness of a bizarre and terrible nature which the organism has itself produced. 'It is nothing other than yourself.'

Gradually, as he works away at his prayer and his loving, the contemplative finds the difficult details of his life fall into place. He stops fussing about minor needs and disappointments and learns to take what comes. He learns how not to strain himself emotionally, and he abandons everything which might be a spiritual affectation. An element of gaiety creeps into his relations with God. He can, if he wishes, says the Cloud, 'have a lovely game with Him' . . . He even, in a way that would make Dale Carnegie envious, becomes more attractive to other people, because suddenly he is 'at home with everyone he talks to'.

Setting the knowledge of the senses on one side, and learning to live 'this nothing in its nowhere' he feels at times that the struggle will destroy him and that 'he might as well be looking at hell for the despair he feels of ever reaching perfection and peace out of all this suffering.' At other times, such is the peace and rest he finds that he thinks he may be in heaven.

These ups and downs are abrasions which prepare the soul for its final and terrible, though longed-for transformation. 'There still remains between you and God the stark awareness of your own existence. And this awareness, too, must go, before you experience contemplation in its perfection.'

Yet it is the peculiar nature of this transformation that it is not something strange to us, but rather it represents our own innermost longing for wholeness, 'For it is not what you are or have been that God looks at with his merciful eyes, but what you would be.'

The *Cloud* has a cheerful Anglo-Saxon sturdiness about it.

Ecstatic heights and depressive depths are described as if they were the most normal thing in the world, and the impression the author gives is of a very balanced man who has used his sanity and wisdom to make a voyage into strange and perilous territory and then to tell others about the pitfalls and joys. He has pitted his slender equipment against the forces of transcendence, and not only survived but triumphed. Even the loneliness and the darkness do not really shake his Crusoe-like adaptability.

For others one may guess that it has been harder. Both the heights and the depths have made more demands on the more sensitive, and those who have been most aware of natural beauty and the natural desires of the body have found the 'forgetting' of creation, of which the Cloud speaks, a path of intense suffering.

St. John of the Cross's careful analysis of his suffering (and of the unspeakable joy of which it is the reverse side) suggest at times a man racked by the torments of his journey, yet possibly racked even more by its beauties and joys. He is a profoundly sensual man — his writing is full of the richest imagery drawn from nature and from the heights of sexual love, yet he seems always to have known that the satisfaction that his senses yearned for was not, for him, to be found among the simple joys of created things, but in the source which lay beyond the creation. The very compulsion of the senses makes his version of the journey more austere and more extreme; troubled by the confusions of imagination he has to be more rigorous than others in setting it on one side and living within the emptiness which it leaves. Darkness and night dominate his understanding of his spiritual journey; since the soul cannot bear the blazing light of God it must learn how to travel, gently and patiently, in darkness, noting the beauties of the night — its scents, soft noises, breezes and stars, but also bearing the desolation which darkness inflicts upon a creature made to see. His spiritual Sentences and Maxims outline, often rather bleakly, the stoniness of the path. 'Love consists not in feeling great things, but in having great detachment and in suffering for the Beloved.'

On this *via negativa* the natural clinging to people and objects must be renounced in favour of a separation which is baffling alike to the senses and the intellect, and the bewilderment caused by this denial brings about the first of the 'Nights' for which St. John was famous — the 'Night of the Senses'.

'This dark night', says St. John,[4] 'is an inflowing of God into the soul, which purges it from its ignorances and imperfections, habitual, natural and spiritual, and which is called by contemplatives infused contemplation. . . .' It is not only that the soul is blind until it has begun to move away from itself and its subjective longings: it is that to begin with its joy is simultaneously its agony.

Just as, the clearer is the light, the more it blinds and darkens the pupil of the owl, and, the more directly we look at the sun, the greater is the darkness which it causes in our visual faculty, overcoming and overwhelming it through its own weakness. In the same way, when this Divine light of contemplation assails the soul which is not yet wholly enlightened, it causes spiritual darkness in it; . . . likewise it overwhelms it and darkens the act of its natural intelligence.

In its bewilderment, darkness, weakness, and guilt, the soul suffers terribly, and genuinely believes at times that it is undergoing death, as, in a sense, it is. 'The soul feels itself to be perishing and melting away . . . even as if it had been swallowed by a beast and felt itself being devoured in the darkness of its belly, suffering such anguish as was endured by Jonah in the belly of that beast of the sea. For in this sepulchre of dark death it must needs abide until the spiritual resurrection which it hopes for.' The soul feels itself consumed in its poverty and aridity. 'The soul must needs be in all respects reduced to a state of emptiness, poverty and abandonment and must be left dry and empty and in darkness. For the sensual part is purified in aridity, the faculties are purified in the emptiness of their apprehensions, and the spirit is purified in thick darkness.'

The soul emerges from this first Dark Night into a new relationship with God — as Professor Allison Peers puts it 'the night of purgation fades into the dawn of the illuminative life'. It is a kind of betrothal state in which the soul guesses, with joy, something of what awaits it. It is joyful, but still in a state of darkness, what Dionysius calls a 'ray of darkness' and what St. John

---

[4] *Complete Works of St. John of the Cross*, tr. E. Allison Peers (Burns Oates, 1953).

calls 'the serene night'. 'It is not as the dark night, but as the night which is already near the rising of the morning . . .'

Yet a more terrible Night awaits the soul as the divine love and light beat more fiercely upon it. Like Herbert the soul perceives that 'none goes that way and lives', at least not as living is generally understood. With nothing left to it but faith, hope and love, the soul stumbles onwards on its journey.

Gradually it moves towards *unio mystica*, or Spiritual Marriage, the soul's transformation in God. 'In glory and in appearance the soul seems to be God, and God the soul.' It has become like a star which reflects the light of the sun.

In describing all this St. John is not talking about what *ought* to happen to every Christian soul. He is saying that it is for those who feel themselves summoned. If they do their best to respond faithfully at every stage of their journey, however painful it may be, then step by step they will find themselves moving away from their initial piety, with its reflection and meditation, and its inevitable concomitant of self-satisfaction, into increasingly self-less states. Many, according to St. John, pass through the 'Night of the Senses' and embark upon the 'serene night' of illumination. Very few reach the deathly Night of the spirit and the transformation which lies on the far side of it.

It would be idle to pretend that Christianity, in any of its traditions, has led or encouraged the majority of its followers into any profound mystical experience. There have been profound mystical movements in all the main streams of Christianity, and in many of the minor streams, but in practice the Churches have seen their role as maintaining a sort of balance, with transcendent experience on one side of the scale and the solid structures of dogma and doctrine on the other. Ritual, and more particularly the ritual of the Mass, has played a curious double role, both leading men in towards the springs of life and of love, yet also 'filtering out' the aspects of transcendence which might possibly pose any threat to their sanity. The dangers have often been obvious enough; yet since there *is* no approach to God without danger, then too great a caution can spell torpor and potential death.

The emphasis on safety has been most damaging for those who are by nature the least daring, which is to say, the least conscious. For those, on the other hand, who have moved onwards from a state of acute consciousness into deep awareness and responsiveness to God then this solid structure of the Church in its various manifestations has been a much-needed home. It has been able to assimilate the most dazzling heights and depths of human experience without surprise or excitement or dismay, and so has been a force on the side of sanity, a light-house encouragingly in view through the most racking tempests.

Certain truths have resonated throughout organised Christianity from its earliest days until now, losing themselves at times like an echo in a dome, but then bounding back to repeat themselves once more. The heart of Christianity lies in one shattering insight which is certainly implicit in other religions, perhaps in every religion, but is explicitly so in Christianity. It is that the heart of the human experience, properly lived, is death, but that this death, faithfully experienced, inevitably yields again to life. The vast majority of Christian followers may have lacked the awareness to embark consciously upon any journey, yet they have never been able to escape the reminder that despair and suffering yield to joy, or that death is the condition of abundant life. This has been taught by Christianity as part of a parallel discovery — that God is the 'inside' of human experience, that Christ is, so to speak, us. Thus, the Christian journey has not been for the faithful alone, nor only for those who, like Bunyan's Christian, set out upon the stony road. It is not, in the final analysis, what we do. It *is* us, and our experience of living. When human experience is dissected we unerringly find the Cross, the Cross of contradiction and of opposites, the Cross of physical and mental suffering and of brutality, the Cross of despair. And as unerringly we find Resurrection. The life of Christ becomes a key to what would otherwise be totally incomprehensible, an insight into a process in which every man is caught up. 'The tragic question which this life poses', writes A. M. Allchin, '. . . can be so dark, so fascinating, so terrifying, that it is only through the prism of the life-giving death on the Cross that we are able to look into it.'[5]

Other Christian insights are buried so deeply in Western culture that we only begin to notice them when they are explicitly denied. Perhaps the most influential has had to do with the 'looking-glass' nature of love, with its far-reaching repercussions upon moral decisions. The preaching of vulnerability, of gentleness, of detachment, and of treating our brother as if he is Christ himself

5 *New Blackfriars*, June, 1970, Vol. 51, No. 601, p. 279.

(or our own self), and the insistence that it is the unlikely route which leads to happiness and fulfilment has a kind of Alice in Wonderland perverseness about it, a perverseness so like life itself that it has helped to persuade many of its essential truth.

Like all religious teaching it has both worked and failed. It has worked in the profound Western emphasis upon the value of the person, and in the social concern which follows from this. Again and again Christian consciences have made men conscious of the harshness of their dealings with their neighbour — the Shaftesburys and Barnardos and Wilberforces and Booths have shone like beacons of justice and concern. It has worked too, in building the family as a working unit within which children could be brought up with tolerable security, both financial and emotional. And it has worked on the apparently simple, but infinitely precious level of building up a kind of stability of society, a stability resting on the fact that such anti-social habits as lying, stealing, cheating, physical violence and sexual excess were frowned upon and permitted only in certain well-recognised circumstances, such as, respectively, certain aspects of business and politics, war and prostitution.

Yet we find ourselves wondering now about the sort of splitting which this has imposed. The very emphasis upon the individual has had a splitting effect, cutting him off from his awareness of himself as part of a moving stream in which he is linked not just with his fellow-men but with the whole process of creation around him. His 'I' becomes not a sweet gift, a kind of instrument with which to participate in the whole created world, but a fortress, from which death is seen as the ultimate surrender and disgrace. The emphasis upon goodness has led to a denial of the parts of ourselves which are not by any stretch of imagination good, and powerful forces, such as aggression, have lurked within, unacknowledged, wreaking a terrible revenge upon ourselves and others. The terror that this has imposed has led to a turning away from the raging cauldrons within into a desperate preoccupation with activity, an activity which, even if directed into works of goodness and of mercy, makes inner growth and self-awareness an impossibility.

Finally, the emphasis on sexual and emotional detachment has made a kind of Procrustean bed for us on which all too easily we have mutilated ourselves. Most of our sexual ethic is pro-

foundly influenced to this day by the sexual needs of a people —
the Jews of Old Testament times — who had a robust and
wonderfully rich erotic imagination. Detachment, physical and
emotional, for people who can live as fully as that, becomes not
a grim asceticism, but a progression, a moving into maturity.
And it can be this, in our own day, for those who are already
mature and fulfilled people.

Yet the signs are there for all to see that sexually most of us
are neither fulfilled nor mature. Our neuroses, our marriage
breakdowns, the dreams with which we sustain ourselves in books
and films and television plays do not reflect people who are erotic-
ally content, nor who have enjoyed deep emotional relationships
with those who are close to them. On the contrary, they offer
their tragic testimony of frustration, of sterile marriages and joyless affairs, of preoccupation with impotence and frigidity, and
of an infantile fascination with violence.

This is not the 'fault' of Christianity, nor of Western man in
any real sense; it is simply the path along which both have
stumbled towards maturity. If we had not made these mistakes
we should have made others, perhaps more serious ones. Mistake is the condition of learning. But what now? Is that particular journey — the journey of the Christian — a closed path
which now leads only to a broken path and a cliff edge? I don't
believe that it is, yet the possibility of growth seems to demand
an inner leap, a kind of evolutionary jump of almost unimagin-
able proportions. The intense provincialism of thought that still
surrounds much Christian thinking — the tacit refusal to step
outside the known framework and simply give ourselves up to the
problems of being a human being, together with the very real fear
that good may come out of the Nazareth of non-Christian thinking, inhibits vision.

The irony of it is that read within the context of the later part
of the twentieth century the Christian gospels seem to have one
most remarkable axe which they grind with an almost merciless
determination, making the other insights, with the exception of
the Passion itself, fade into insignificance. It is that the Christian
journey, perhaps the only journey, is to face the truth, and act
upon it. Beside this single, remorseless demand for self-awareness,
repeated over and over again in various forms in Christ's innumerable encounters with the sick and the sad, the successful and the

powerful, much else in the gospels seems to fade into the background. Even the nine lepers, who had more excuse than most people for giving themselves up to rapturous joy, and for not asking too many questions about how they got healed, are criticised by Christ for their crass blindness. No amount of healing, no pious exercise, no act of charity, will do instead of the agonising journey of self-awareness, since no other path leads to God.

Part II

CHAPTER FIVE

Seventies' Journey

THE STRUGGLES FOR JOURNEY IN OUR OWN TIME MIGHT BE SEEN
as taking place in one or other of two frameworks. Within one
framework the structures of society are still taken for granted;
within the other part of what the journey demands is a destruction of those structures and the fixed ideas which accompany
them.

Those who make their journey within the structures find what
they need for spiritual growth in the traditional framework of
marriage and family life and within a democratic and capitalist
society. They may or may not be involved with Christianity, but
they find enough conflict and satisfaction in personal relations
and in work to have a sense of movement, not to be overcome by
either boredom or despair. Political or social involvement, a
sense of dedication to humanity by means of their job, or some
profound experience such as psychoanalysis or a knowledge of the
arts keeps them aware of what it is to be human.

There is nothing new about any of this; most of these methods
have been part of man's spiritual journey for centuries, though
they are threatened now by the revolutionary spirit of our times.
Most of this chapter is not about the traditional journey, although
many people still follow it, since so much has already been written
about this. It is an attempt to see something about the journey
of those who have chosen the alternative method of working outside the usual structures, in fact the 'alternative society'.

So far the 'alternative society' is anarchic, inimical to our
settled society and its ways, and though it has strong religious
elements these owe very little to the Christianity traditional in
these islands. It is remarkable so far for the changes it has effected

in the visual quality of our lives, but it has also challenged our perceptions in other ways; one of its notable effects has been its assault on the human senses.

It has affected dress, aesthetic standards, sexual codes, living habits, food and vocabulary, producing changes at a lightning speed. Its most enthusiastic supporters are those under thirty. It is still in a state of flux and shows signs of being in an early stage of its development; it remains to be seen how successfully it will engulf such a long-established and conformist society as our own.

People sometimes refer to this alternative movement as 'hippies', but the hippie period is long past. The hippies were possibly the most naive group that the alternative movement is likely to throw up, and perhaps because of the *naïveté* (according to some observers) were brutally smashed. The hippies were at their peak in the mid-sixties, and were bravely dedicated to the idea of living without work and without money. An observer of one hippie commune in the Balls Pond Road described how they managed to live a mendicant existence. This produced a degree of poverty unusual in the West, and meant begging spare food from hotels, picking up fruit and vegetables, which had dropped out of the boxes in Covent Garden, straightforward begging, possibly some stealing. They also fed off other people's charity — one week they lived on a sack of onions which someone gave them — but sometimes they made money by singing.

The members of the commune were a shifting group of men and women aged between sixteen and forty. In the course of six months around 200 people had slept in the house and had a greater or lesser involvement with its life. Members believed, at least at first, in a total sexual freedom, though they suffered conflict, according to my observer, because of feelings of jealousy which seemed inappropriate to a free sexual ethic.

Their end was a sad and unexpected one. As time went on they began to attract more and more interest from the press, which in turn led to their becoming something of a curiosity to the public. The extreme poverty which had proved a powerful bond for the group was relieved by various kinds of financial help, and finally a very wealthy patron took them up, giving large sums of money not to the commune as a whole but to individual members. Some of these disappeared on wild Continental holidays and the subsequent strains and rows finally split the whole enterprise.

That kind of mendicant group seems largely to have disappeared. 'You can't afford poverty in this society!' one member of the Underground remarked when I asked if poverty were an ideal among any of his friends, and the taste in dress, housing, and motor cars among the intelligent young who are able to earn money is far from cheap.

But if poverty (at least of the voluntary sort) has gone, the sense of the importance of the group, and the group experience, has not. 'All sixteen-year-olds want to live in a commune' a member of the staff of 'Release' told me. She felt that for them it represented an idealised family, offering the warmth and love of family life without the conflict with their parents. Few actually do live in a commune at that age. A year or two later, however, many young people do come to London to live and work. They take a bed-sitting room in a district like Notting Hill but after a fortnight are liable to be turned out by their landlord, because so many other youngsters have piled in to share it with them. Slightly older people also find themselves living in a group, not necessarily voluntarily. 'People are often *forced* to live in a commune' said 'Release', pointing out the many young couples in London who are obliged to share houses with other families because of the shortage of accommodation.

This kind of compulsory commune is rather different from the commune by choice. These range from groups with some particular religious or social ideal to families who feel it cheaper and more labour-saving to live with other people. The commune experience, 'Release' claim, can be desperately disillusioning for the most idealistic, brutally introducing them to hard facts about their relationships with others which in other circumstances might pass undiscovered. Those who found relationships most difficult were sometimes those most attracted by the idea. Some of the really tough experiences were had by those who tried to set up self-supporting communities — growing all their own food, making their own clothes, etc. Such experiences were good for those who could survive, but they tended to be people who would get along well in most situations.

Of course, communes are not a new idea, even in this century. Many communes were set up in the twenties and thirties, some of which are still in existence, and some of these have assimilated a new generation of *communards*.

According to 'Release' much of the impetus of the alternative society derives from the fact that urban life in this country has become so intolerable that the need to make it livable breaks through the crust of traditional conformity. The psychedelic revolution has been, amongst other things, a cry of despair. A new way of living, a new approach to sex, were to be derived from new insights, and the new insights in turn derived from being 'turned on' by ecstatic experience. 'Turning on' was to be achieved, is achieved, by drugs, meditation, sex, music, and these roads to the unconscious are intended to outline a new kind of journey. They also form a particular kind of response to a highly conscious rational and manipulative kind of society, and members of the Underground tend to be hostile to a scientific and technological approach to the human situation. This is strikingly demonstrated by what happened at a comprehensive school in Hampstead. They had been accustomed to have around one hundred sixth form members studying science, but the numbers shrank dramatically to two after the psychedelic revolution reached their pupils; the numbers have continued to be low.

Who are the members of the alternative society? They are in the main under thirty, and they tend to feel their youthfulness as an important part of the cult. 'You will show to the world that your generation, which appears to be listening with every courtesy, is in fact deaf,' as the defendants said to the judge at the *Oz* trial. In London they are to be found in Notting Hill, and in the districts farther out, sometimes called the West London Village. Outside London, nearly every city, and certainly every University, has its Underground. Moreover, it is an international movement, and the Continent, America, Canada, Australia and New Zealand all have enthusiastic members. In England it is essentially middle-class, though some of their inspiration derives from working-class sources, such as the Beatles. There is a strong public school element among them — 'Scratch a hippie and find a public school boy,' one clergyman said to me when I asked about his experience in hippie groups, going on to suggest that far from being the passive and inadequate personality which public opinion often imagined the hippie to be, hippies had often shown extreme initiative and enterprise in escaping from their background and changing their way of life. Yet others, including those who are members of the alternative society, complain of the way that inadequate personalities who find it hard to cope with a job or with personal relationships, easily drift into undemanding attitudes of protest and dissent.

Yet many intelligent young people who are perfectly well able to hold down decently paid jobs in the established society would also want to be counted as members of the Underground. The guilt that some of them feel about taking money from a society they despise and wish to destroy is eased by the thought that the jobs they do may be of key-importance in changing the attitudes of society. As journalists, television directors, writers, lecturers in politics or sociology, they can have a profound influence on the way people think. Others are again employed within the new society, in arts labs, or on the innumerable little papers of the Underground. Others work only when driven by the need for money, taking up one of the many casual jobs which big cities offer.

Apart from those who have more or less broken with the old middle-class way of life, however, there are many more who manage to keep a foot in both camps, following the habits of the new society — growing their hair, wearing unusual clothes, enjoying rock, drugs, and a permissive attitude to sex — while keeping within the acceptable limits of the old society. Many are young people who live at home and are holding down a conventional job, or studying with a view to holding down a conventional job.

At first glance the most remarkable change the alternative society has achieved is in people's appearance. The cult of long, flowing hair for both men and women has spread far beyond the young, becoming a tacit way of expressing sympathy with the new movement. The short, tidy, permed style for women, or the short back and sides for men, has become an indication of the 'uptightness' of the wearer, and of implicit hostility to dramatic social change. Other changes in dress also suggest a movement away from rigidity; women who have been influenced by the new trends are no longer corseted, and men no longer wear heavily padded suits with a collar and tie. The changes suggest not just freedom but also defencelessness; women's bodies are covered by fewer garments, and those they have make no attempt to conceal or even improve upon, their natural curves. Men are not buttoned up behind waistcoats. Either sex can undress in a matter of seconds.

The movement does not seem to be towards provocation — suspenders, sheer stockings, high heels, tight lacing, pointed bras, have all been killed by the movement — but rather towards the kind of naturalness about the body which made it possible for young mothers at Woodstock to suckle their babies in public.

Dress has many features which have long been common to bohemian costume — long skirts, unusual patterned fabrics, sandals, wide-brimmed hats, velvet jackets. There is an old-fashioned, romantic quality about it which seems to hark back to many aesthetic movements in Europe in the last two hundred years, and which is as far removed as possible from the ideas of *couturier* elegance or 'smartness' which was the post-war ideal in women's dress. The *hauteur* and the disdainful mannequin's walk which marked that particular style have been swept away in favour of a gayer and more spontaneous way of being a woman. One style suggested untouchability, frigidity; the other suggests its opposite.

Men's clothes have changed even more dramatically than women's. Young men have aroused hostility in the older generation because they have adopted features of dress which had been regarded as feminine — flowered fabrics, or fabrics in pastel colours.

Perhaps the greatest heresy against the *couturier* elegance on which the older generation were brought up is that clothes are often meant to be funny, satirical, or light-hearted. Young men may dress in old military uniforms to express their ridicule of soldiers; women will wear funny hats or garments just because it expresses some light-hearted whim. Clothes, and by implication the bodies inside them, are no longer to be treated with grave solemnity, nor as potentially dangerous indicators of our sillier or more unstable traits. They have become a personal form of art, a picture we draw for those around us on a canvas we have always to hand.

The essence of Underground dress is the idea of play, an idea developed at length by Richard Neville in *Play Power*.[1] By play, according to Neville, the world is to be transformed. In civilised

[1] Richard Neville, *Play Power* (Cape, 1970).

society we have caught ourselves in an intolerable trap. With our nine to five jobs, our suburban matchboxes of homes, our rigid educational system, our obsessions with status and with substitute sex, our compulsive overworking, we have made our lives virtually intolerable, and it is no wonder that we are so vulnerable to mental illness, physical collapse, and the attractions of suicide, in all its forms from addiction and car accidents to taking overdoses of pills.

For Neville the alternative is to turn work into play (which he claims the Underground presses and organisations have succeeded in doing), to recover our childlike awareness of sensual delights, to 'turn on' to sex, as well as other forms of ecstasy, and, most important of all, since most of the other reforms ultimately depend on it, to 'fuck the system'.

Because 'play' sounds such an amiable and harmless pursuit, it is easy to overlook just how revolutionary the Underground movement is, a movement which, potentially at least, could turn out to be as explosive as the Reformation. It aims at intensifying contempt for and disillusion in the 'system' together with, except for those in self-supporting communes, which is very few, living off it. A recent television broadcast was advising the young to stay at home (that is to live off the parents who are bound in the old system) until they were quite sure that they were in a position to make it alone in the big city, though they were also advised to work on the task of 'radicalizing their parents and neighbourhoods'. Neville himself, coolly, and indeed very entertainingly, advises his readers in techniques of sponging, cadging and downright stealing as the way to keep going through the leaner phases of play.

'Play' is not a bad summing up of the contemporary attempt to find a journey, and if it sounds deceptively trivial then this is to mistake the nature of what is being said. What is being urged is the rediscovery of the body, the rediscovery of community, and the rediscovery of (in a sense) religious faith.

Our response to this call to a journey must depend upon how unsatisfactory and doomed we feel the present organisation of society to be, or whether we are advocating some other form of radical change, say Marxism, which we feel would do the job better. If, despite doubts and discomforts, we are basically happy with existing society, then we can only feel resentful

about movements like play power, and become increasingly
paranoid about their willingness to take from a society to which
they are not prepared to contribute, at least in the obvious ways.
Even if we are not all that happy, we may have great difficulty
in imagining any other way of life really succeeding, especially
one that is not based upon the rock of hard work and a firm
sexual ethic; we have been heavily conditioned to regard work
as a virtue, and to feel that retribution overtakes those (oh, that
Roman Empire!) who do what they please. Or we may feel that
we have so much invested in the present society as it is, that
change is too difficult for us. The way we were brought up and
educated, and the way we toiled at our jobs, has been too costly
for us idly to abandon our painful adjustment.

Or we may have real sympathy with what the movement is
fighting for, and a hope that at least some of its ideas will permeate our institutions and society, while distrusting something
brutal and heartless in the inability to see the cost of revolution.
The unspoken slogan behind every revolution is that in order to
make people happy it doesn't matter if you make them wretchedly
miserable. If they are wretchedly miserable enough before the
revolution starts you may argue that they could not be much
worse off and you may be right, but in our own very complex
situation in which the misery is not necessarily the obvious
kind, it is more difficult.

Nevertheless, play power could not have succeeded as it has
if there was not a widespread need to realise its objectives, especially among the young, and whether or not it succeeds in the rapid
overthrow of our institutions, or whether it follows a slower route
of infiltration, there seems little doubt that many of its insights
will permeate our thinking and our way of life as they have
already begun to do.

In the enormous pop festivals, in the discos, in the communes,
in the tribal mood which dominated a musical like *Hair* we can
sense a longing for community — a community more accepting,
more loving, and also much more honest than the communities, or
pseudo-communities, that most of us have grown up in. 'How
can people be so heartless?' sings the girl in *Hair*. 'I need a
friend ... I need a friend.' The community envisaged leaps over
racial differences, and over sexual differences, in the sense of
deviations. It is very tolerant of drug-taking. It would like to leap

over the generation gap, but finds this more difficult because the
older generation appear as persecutors, mocking at long hair,
envious of sexual freedom, criticising dress and values, turning
young men into soldiers (as in *Hair*) and sending them to war.

A successful community, the life-style of the young seems to
be asserting, depends upon the sharing of whatever one has, upon
not being too pernickety and perfectionist about one's living
standards, and above all, upon absence of fear. So many of our
moral and legal ideas seem based on the assumption that our
neighbour, given half a chance, is bound to take advantage of us.
It is as if rape, physical or financial, was never far from our minds.
But if property and wealth is kept at a minimum, and in any case
freely shared with one's 'mates', and if one's body is similarly
not seen as a private sanctum, but rather as an instrument of
relationship, then, so runs the unspoken argument, the fear
disappears, and with it the need to see one's neighbour as an
enemy.

To an older generation this is almost as startling in its bearing upon property as it is about sex; it is almost impossible not
to view it in terms of the penalties and pains such an attitude
used to exact. It is not easy to arrive at the inner freedom from
which to consider the sexual/communal revolution on its merits,
nor to admit that the strongest argument against may be that *we*
have not lived like that.

Nevertheless the change is far-reaching, and whatever the
inevitable areas of destruction, there is also an undeniable
honesty and cheeriness about it.

There is a change in sexual style. A shift in the structure of
human relationships. Seduction is obsolete. According to the
Shorter Oxford Dictionary to 'seduce' means to tempt, entice
or beguile someone to do wrong.... The prospect of having
to 'tempt, beguile or entice' today's freewheeling girls to bed
is, well... Underground sexual morality is, in its own way,
as direct as the Old Testament. If a couple like each other,
they make love. Table for two, boxes of chocolates, saying it
with flowers, cementing it with diamonds — seem as dated as
Terry Thomas in a smoking jacket.... One cannot offer veri-
fying statistics. The sons of Kinsey have not yet emerged from
their Underground researches to disclose that hippiedom is

Peyton Place without the lies or Polynesia without the super-
stitions — but they will. . . . And yet it is not promiscuity . . .
which is significant. It could just be possible that the sexual
candour of the radical generation is indicative of a healthier,
more honest overall relationship, the longing for which was
naively embodied in that ridiculed anti-warcry 'All you Need
is Love'.[2]

What is gone is the acute shame which once went with admitting the strength and variety of the sexual appetite. 'The randy
skeleton is removed from the cupboard and hung trophy-like over
the fire-place', as Neville colourfully puts it. 'It's groovy to be
carnal. And there's nothing more carnal than the Underground,
although to communicate its unique sexual atmosphere is like
trying to teach a blind man to play hopscotch.'

In Neville's own writing the unique atmosphere is evident in
the total lack of guilt and fear, and this is an enviable achievement shared by many of his fellow radicals. His comparison of
the uptight businessmen watching stag-shows in Soho, and a
younger generation who have no patience with such spectator
sports, is a telling one.

That the Underground generation are sexually freer than their
forebears is not in doubt. What we don't yet know is whether
sexuality freed from the deep and rigid channels Western morality cut for it is able to achieve any sort of synthesis with love, nor
whether that is even expected of it any longer. Vancouver's
Georgia Straight suggests that on the far side of promiscuity
lies the discovery that relationship is what matters.

Chances are that you will attend three or four more parties.
You will feel more relaxed at the next ones, and eventually try
most of the things you have heard, dreamed or read about.
You will forget to ask names and may not even think twice
about sleeping with someone you don't know anything about
much less have any feeling for. You will find that you can still
have sexual fantasies and that V.D. is easily taken care of.
Chances of lasting friendships are rare. You will still have
most of your sexual and emotional hang-ups and maybe a few
new ones. The hang-ups of the people you will meet may be

2 Ibid.

worse. You will be more sexually aware and you certainly will
be jaded to a certain extent. With relief, you will go back to
sex on a private basis, not sorry that you participated in the
'scene', but feeling somewhat about 'organized sex' as you do
about 'organized religion'.

What is evident in these descriptions of the sexual scene is how
the attitudes of women have changed. They no longer need to be
seduced, but can be expected to decide for themselves what they
want to do about sex; nor is there any suggestion that virginity
is prized nor fidelity expected. What is not mentioned by Neville
at all is sexual jealousy which has in the past perhaps been the
strongest reason for the rigidity of our sexual ideas and for the
lies which have surrounded sexual exploits.

Can people know and not mind if those they love have sexual
relations with others? If they don't mind, is this because they
have freed themselves from a conditioning which makes those
we love or marry 'our' property, or is it because they have repressed their anger and hurt, or did not have a deep relationship
in the first place? This is not a rhetorical question meant as an
attack on the Underground. I believe the answers are very
important, but that whatever our prejudices at the moment we
don't really know the answers because we *are* conditioned, conditioned especially by our own investment in society and in
relationships.

If the prurience of our society (as evinced in newspapers, films,
paperbacks, strip clubs, etc.) is anything to go by then we have so
far failed, and failed pitiably, in achieving any true synthesis of
sex and love. It seems very possible that a greater freedom in
realising sexual fantasies, and above all in loosening the bonds
of guilt which tend to aggravate sexual problems, might lead to
greater sexual satisfaction and happiness. But we have a long
way to go before we are prepared to surrender our guilt, and no
doubt will have to digest very much more 'permissiveness' than
we have seen so far, assimilating such polymorphously perverse
items as the illustrations to *Oz*, to make the uncomfortable discovery that parts of us are still infantile. This is not a happy
discovery for most adults — middle-aged women in particular
resenting such awareness and so tending to ally themselves with
puritanical movements — so that the battle between the movement

with its cheery insistence that fucking is a good thing, and the opposition, for whom it can only be considered within marriage, shows signs of being a violent one.

The other prong of the puritan attack is directed at the drug-taking of the movement, and since the drug-scene is complex and confused, and we have had little time in which to develop a reliable folk-lore about drugs and how to take them (as we have long ago done about alcohol), then they have been particularly successful in fostering anxiety among teachers, parents, and establishment figures.

The ostensible anxiety is that the young will become hooked on one drug or another, and under its influence will become anti-social, sexually irresponsible, lazy about work, and finally will 'drop-out'. The other anxiety is that in the search for drugs, they will fall into bad company, that of 'pushers' who are eager to sell dangerous drugs, and will be led into bad ways and corrupted against their will. Occasional television documentaries and news-paper articles do paint very horrifying pictures of junkies.

This is not the place to examine the dangers of drug-taking, but only the extent to which it is, and is seen by those who take part to be, part of a journey or spiritual quest. Two drugs are considered to be relevant to spirituality by the young of the Underground, pot and LSD (together with drugs of a similar effect to LSD such as mescalin, psylobycin, peyote, etc.).

Pot produces a pleasantly relaxed feeling, a feeling of friendli-ness, and an enhanced enjoyment of music and painting. Except possibly for experienced takers, it is very much less powerful and definite in effect than alcohol, in fact it is an exceedingly mild drug. It is used by many as an aid to receptivity — receptivity to music or other arts, receptivity to meditative and contemplative experiences, and in so far as a quietening of the body and mind is needed before it is possible to embark on these, then it has a particular value, particularly for those whose minds and bodies have to function in a very active society.

In so far as quietness, reflectiveness, contemplation, and enjoy-ment of the arts help in a general relaxing of attitudes of life, and an awareness that immediate anxieties and desires are not the whole truth about it, then pot does in the end become a sort of antidote to excessive busyness, ambition, and an ego-centred life, but it would probably have to be taken over a long period

by someone who was already seeking to balance their personality
in that way to be really effective. All the same it makes a telling
symbol of what the younger generation are searching for, and is
a shaming reminder to those who smoke or drink too much that
one's pleasures and habits can be directed towards growth rather
than to simple dependence.

I do not think anyone would claim that pot produces any very
startling spiritual experiences, but rather that it deepens awareness and enjoyment of one's surroundings, and is a sort of pre-
paration for a deeper communion with life, as relaxing in an
armchair before the fire might be the first stage in intimate conversation with a friend.

LSD and similar drugs are a totally different experience,
constituting for probably the majority of takers, a journey in themselves. William James, experimenting with nitrous oxide in 1902,
was plunged into an experience which many taking LSD have
since experienced themselves. 'Looking back on my own experiences they all converge towards a kind of insight to which
I cannot help ascribing some metaphysical significance. The key
note of it is invariably a reconciliation. It is as if the opposites of
the world, whose contradictoriness and conflict makes all our
difficulties and troubles, were melted into unity.'[3]

This astonishing description can be repeated in innumerable
forms by other takers of psychedelic drugs. The psychiatrist
R. D. Laing describes LSD as giving a 'meta-egoic' experience,
and Timothy Leary calls it a 'spiritual challenge'. 'Marijuana is
the perfect drug to make you feel better, but ... LSD requires
a change of mind.' And Richard Neville, never a man for anything fancy or high-falutin', says that LSD 'transforms the mun-
dane into the sensational'.

Not everyone would agree with these judgments. R. C.
Zaehner, Spalding Professor of Eastern Religions and Ethics
at Oxford, has described a desperately trivial, indeed ludicrous,
experience he had under LSD, but it is difficult not to feel from
his writing that he wanted it that way, and with psychedelic
drugs, as with sex, the mood and the expectation with which
they are entered upon may be of crucial importance. If you seek
triviality you find it. If you want to re-experience events from
early childhood, and are helped by an attendant psychiatrist

[3] William James, *The Varieties of Religious Experience* (Fontana, 1971).

to do so, you stand a good chance of succeeding. If you long for spiritual enlightenment, for some inkling of God, some message of the meaningfulness of the world, then this too you are likely to get, perhaps rather more completely than you bargained for. Such drugs tend to yield experiences copiously, related to birth and death, to suffering and joy, to good and evil, to God and the Devil, to heaven and hell, quite apart from illuminating ordinary objects — wallpaper, furniture, clothes, flowers, curtains, in the most astonishing way. For those *not* on a journey, who have happened upon acid by chance, or to be fashionable, then the unfamiliar inner landscape is hostile, horrifying and dangerous. This appears very vividly in two books about Mexico by an American sociologist Carlos Castenada.[4] Asked why he does not give *Mescalito* (mescalin) to his grandson Lucio, a boy who has no thought for anything beyond motor-bikes and American fashions, the wise old Don Juan replies that in his present state of mind it would kill him. It is a tragic feature of unsupervised drug-taking that so many have stumbled upon visions for which nothing had prepared them and which they did not want.

There are other problems too about LSD in a society which not only has no folk-lore about drug-taking but has no lively mystical tradition into which transcendent and archetypal experiences could be calmly and wisely absorbed. Some turn to gurus and Buddhist teachers for help and advice, and often find it, though advice which is filtered to one through a foreign background and culture may lack depth of mutual communication just where it would be most useful. Critical judgment is especially valuable to people seeking spiritual advice, and it is difficult to employ it against someone who, superficially at least, is very different from oneself. Some turn to monks or nuns, to clergy, or to psychoanalysts for help. There are individuals in all these groups who can give what is needed, but they are not easy to find (there are very few of them), and very few have themselves travelled widely enough in the inner space to have got beyond prejudices and a nervous clinging to a theoretical framework which will not necessarily be relevant.

The greatest problem about LSD, however, is to do with

4 Carlos Castenada, *The Teachings of Don Juan: Yaqui Way of Knowledge* (Penguin, 1972), and *A Separate Reality: Further Conversations with Don Juan* (Bodley Head, 1971).

perspective. Most of us have become inured to plodding on with our daily lives, to accepting the round of work and family, to earning money, and nodding to the sacred cows with whom we were brought up. Suddenly, given a drug of this type, we have a glimpse of what is needed for wholeness, of what timelessness and transcendence mean. We are in touch with the roots of our being, as we were for a few years in early childhood, before the need to adjust ourselves to society became desperate, and as perhaps we may be on our death-bed. It is as if we have been lifted from the view of an ant on an ant-heap to the perspective of a man who can see the ant-heap for what it is, a tiny mound in a landscape which includes the sky and the fields and the trees.

Once having been shown this wider view it is not easy to go back to caring about our pension, or our rise, our new car, or which party gets in at the next election, and for a while at least this makes the acid-head a deeply subversive influence. None of the usual carrots work for him, since he knows that *sub specie aeternitatis* they will not be of the slightest importance, and he becomes impervious to all the kinds of propaganda — political, national, commercial, social, educational or religious — with which we are all accustomed to be fed. He is as indifferent as a medieval hermit to such incitements.

Unfortunately, he may not be as free as a medieval hermit of responsibilities towards dependents and others, and viewing life on an unnaturally large time scale he may be led into actions (giving up his job, for instance) which can be destructive for his family.

This is not, however, a matter for the easy superiority non-takers often assume. There is courage in taking acid as part of a quest, and it is sometimes by losing ourselves that we find what we were looking for; who is to say that this in the end will be more damaging to our children than a blind conformity to social patterns? Perhaps for some people explosive methods are the only way to growth, at least in a society where contemplative attitudes have been despised. It may be important for society that some people are prepared to restore the balance we have lost in this way.

Nevertheless, the double vision involved puts strain on the individual, and it takes judgment for him to see the risk of allowing himself too large a helping of eternity. One or two trips may be all that he can take without gambling with his everyday humanness.

One of the criticisms made against LSD, by the guru Meyer Baba amongst others, is that it leads takers to imagine that they have reached an advanced stage of spiritual development when actually they are the merest beginners. Because a trip may be full of images of wholeness, they think they are already whole. The experience of seeing natural objects transformed, or of innumerable whirling mandalas, of having deep perceptions about one's companions or about people who are not present, of feeling that one is Buddha or Christ, is enough to unsettle anyone. We are all of us near enough to megalomania to fall into errors of belief about our own importance, our own 'specialness', and men to whom religious symbols are important always tread a difficult and dangerous path in this respect.

But this is not a conclusive argument against taking LSD, at least in a supervised setting, but is rather a sign of our need to develop a new language and a new lore (though much of it will turn out to be very old) about spirituality. Both God-awareness, and a sense of ordinariness are important ingredients, to establish meaning and direction on the one hand, and sanity on the other. Most of us, with or without the help of drugs, are liable to lose sight of one or the other or both, and perhaps should be more grateful than we are to those who can show us either conviction, even if they are lacking in the ideal balance.

Inevitably there are those who cannot bear the thought that mystical experiences can come to men simply through taking a drug. After fasting, sleeplessness, sensory deprivation, yes. After swallowing chemicals, no. There seems to be fear behind this attitude, fear that the visions of the mystics will turn out to be meaningless if their experiences cease to be the privilege of an élite, and anyone can join in.

On one level it is easy to show that their contention is nonsense. Man is a chemical animal, and however unconsciously saints and mystics may have embarked on ascetic practices they were extraordinarily shrewd at hitting upon methods which by inducing chemical changes or mental confusion made supranormal states much more likely. Their methods were slower, cruder, more uncomfortable, but they were methods none the less, and some of them, such as fasting, were regarded almost as *de rigueur*.

All the same there *is*, or seems to be, a difference between a life lived solely as a spiritual quest, with the body trained almost on military lines to an obedience to the spirit, and a life in which there is room for all kinds of excursions into the delights of the senses.

But perhaps what is instructive about the psychedelic drugs is that they will have none of this division between the spiritual and the others. A man with a developed sensuality is as likely to be favoured as a man of prayer. A scatterbrained adolescent can be rewarded with a beatific state, while a professor of religion can be passed over. It is as upsetting to the established order of things as the Magnificat. To the drugs it seems that all ecstasy is one — religious ecstasy, aesthetic ecstasy, sexual ecstasy, are inseparable one from another. There is no higher and lower, no better and worse, no élite. At any one moment, any of us may be, or not be, on our journey, and who we are does not come into it.

If we could develop a folk-lore about such things instead of trying to stop them or ignore them, then perhaps the information we should need to hand to one another and to our children is that such visions are the merest beginning. They are infinitely precious, and they contain in germ the wholeness that we need — that is how we know they are genuine. But better things lie in store for us and we must learn how to experience them in sobriety, which is harder than doing so in intoxication, until the most ordinary of moments and of objects become illuminated.

But perhaps the young know that already. One very influential part of the Underground scene — that of pop — has been full of the awareness of acid. Songs describing trips, making puns on tripping, and turning on, or simply brimming with the sort of imagery peculiar to acid, have become common parlance, yet we have not seen, even among those subjected to special temptations like the Beatles, any sign of megalomania. On the contrary, there have been signs of a growth in love, humility and compassion for mankind.

In the tripping sequence of *Hair*, written out of a burning sense of outrage against conscription for the Vietnam war, the theme is the beauty of man and of the world, and of the horror of destruction. 'How can they dare to end such beauty?'

Marc Bolan, teen-age idol, and star of the T. Rex group describes, in the rather turgid prose of the pop world, the spiritual journey as he sees it.

> Christ must have been a gas. I think he was a very turned-on guy, and very much with God. God is the coolest thing of all. I think if I'm just a splinter out of his head, then he must be a bit like me, not much though. I see him as a monster sun that opens in the middle and you could get sucked into it and out the other side. Where you come out, I don't know, that's only my imagery. But it's a preparation for birth. We're only people and that's a bit of a drag . . . You are born and born again until you reach the ultimate, until you reach another scene, get into another dimension.[5]

But if there is a lack of intellectual content and discipline in pop music that is not very important since what matters is the music itself. At its best this is disciplined, subtle, deeply poetic in feeling, and since it does not depend on words and the barriers they create, it assists the feeling of 'togetherness' and of community which the young are pleading for. It transcends the barriers of country and race, making a kind of *lingua franca*. Ear-drums splitting with the tribal beat of rock, bodies moving to its compulsive rhythms, individuals cease to worry about the problems of communication, or about the clarity of the intellect and of words. What has happened is a kind of Africanisation of cerebral, inhibited European man; he has found a path back into the body and into its spontaneous rhythms, and in doing so has set on one side the problems of identity and the agonies of Kierkegaardian self-awareness. There is not even the sense of guilt and defiance of a D. H. Lawrence. The young have simply turned away from the torturing dilemmas of their parents and chosen another path.

Pop music outlines the path with love and often with delicacy. Despite the novelties of the music itself many of the themes are the staples of all popular music. Romantic love between the

---

[5] Quoted in *Pastoral Care and the Drug Scene*, Kenneth Leech (S.P.C.K., 1970).

sexes is as important a theme now as it has ever been, which is
worth a little thought from those who fear, or hope, that the
contemporary scene is one of unbridled lust. Religious sentiment
(though with certain differences) is as common now as it was
in Victorian and Edwardian ballads; in this respect there is a
real break with the popular music of the past twenty or thirty
years during which religious songs almost disappeared. What is
really quite new (apart from some cheery/satirical songs of the
1914/18 war such as 'I don't want to be a soldier, I don't want
to go to war'), is the song of pacifism, and, underpinning the
pacifism, a sense of love for, and unity with, all mankind. Popular
music has gone international, savouring mankind in all his varia-
tion. Old projections of wickedness, familiar to previous
generations, have been withdrawn, and no one at least within
the charmed circle of the music hates his coloured, Jewish, or
foreign neighbour any more. On the contrary. All the same, there
is still a 'Them', and the 'Them' is now authority, the authority
which sends young men to fight, or which tries to tell them
how to live, or which pushes them around at demonstrations.
'Them' is Nixon, Heath, the school or university authorities, the
system, the police, parents.

There is also social comment — studies of loneliness, suicide,
the rich and the poor — and what is striking is the charity
and the classlessness. There is none of the self-consciousness with
which even a sensitive writer like Orwell could approach the
human condition in the thirties. There are no longer two races
of men, but only one race, and people are either traitors to it,
like 'Them', or they are dedicated to it.

At worst this leads to a note of pretentiousness as the young
lecture their elders about the Third World or urban loneliness,
or reveal sentimentality at the death of young men as in
Seeger's 'Where have all the flowers gone?', (an impoverished
echo of 'The Lament after Flodden'), but at best there is passionate feeling, as in many of Bob Dylan's songs, or in Joan Baez's
'Just a little boy', or in the Beatles' beautifully felt and written
'She's leaving home'.

The note of despair at human callousness emerges as perhaps
it has not done in popular music for centuries, a cry from the
heart of alienated man.

> Isn't it a pity,
> Isn't it a shame,
> How we break each other's hearts, and cause each other pain
> How we take each other's love, Without
>   thinking any more
> Forgetting to give back
> Isn't it a pity?[6]

Hair had already struck this particular note in the song 'How can people be so heartless'.

There is a new sympathy for the differences between people, and the way these have been used to wound and destroy. The Paul Simon song 'He was a most peculiar man' outlines the fate of a man allowed to die of loneliness in a bed-sitting room just because all his life he had been, and felt himself to be 'a most peculiar man'.

Love between the sexes is seen as having, at best, a revelatory quality, before which simplicity and humility are the only possible response.

> Though you sit in another chair I can
>   feel you here.
> Looking like I don't care, but I do, I do —
> Hiding it all behind anything I see, should
>   someone be looking at me.
>
> Let it down — let it down
> Let your hair hang all around me,
> Let it down — let it down — let your love
>   flow and astound me.[7]

The extraordinary naturalness and tough-minded tenderness which the Beatles showed when writing of love between men and women was carried over, without a trace of embarrassment, to their treatment of universal love, and in particular of religious themes. 'All you need is love', though often derided for its simplification of the issues confronting mankind, produced sentiments, freshly minted, which can be found in some of the greatest mystics:

[6] George Harrison, 'All Things Must Pass' (Apple Records).
[7] Ibid.

Nothing you can know that isn't known,
Nothing you can see that isn't shown
Nowhere you can be that isn't where you're meant to be,
S'easy.[8]

George Harrison in particular went on to reveal a genuine mystical vision, a vision which included hunger for God, joyous faith, penitence and humility, and finally, and most movingly, the realisation of the detachment which is part of spiritual freedom.

Sunrise doesn't last all morning
A cloudburst doesn't last all day
Seems my love is up, and has left you with no warning
But it's not always going to be this grey
All things must pass, all things must pass away.

Now the darkness only stays at night time
In the morning it will fade away
Daylight is good at arriving at the right time
No it's not always going to be this grey
All things must pass, all things must pass away.[9]

Harrison's faith is not a specifically Christian one, and it has none of the evangelical fervour and the social conformity with which a Cliff Richard lends himself to ecclesiastical exploitation. Harrison refers easily to Jesus in a song, obviously derived from the Hare Krishna movement, in which he describes spiritual freedom as being available for those who are 'chanting the names of the Lord'.

If you open up your heart, then you will
see he's right there
He always was and will be.

His spirituality has a way of penetrating hypocrisy, 'Beware of Maya' he tells his listeners.

8 The Beatles, 'All you need is Love' (Northern Songs).
9 'All Things Must Pass'.

> Watch out now take care, beware of greedy leaders
> They'll take you where you should not go.

He is not advocating formal religion, but a turning of the heart.

> You don't need no church house, and you
>   don't need no Temple
> And you don't need no rosary beads or
>   them books to read
> To know that you have fallen,
> If you open up your heart then you will
>   know what I mean
> We've been kept down so long
> Someone's thinking that we're all green.

For Harrison the journey has passed beyond protest and indignation to the discovery of inner riches and truth. Apart from a brief reference to the burning out of desire there is little tension in him between body and spirit, or between sexual love and the spiritual kind, only an awareness of the perishability of human life and emotion, and a discovery that what he wants to learn is what he calls in one song 'The Art of Dying'.

The golden goodness and wisdom of the Beatles becomes something darker and more bitter in the hands of the Rolling Stones, a vision of evil, and a blind rage against it. When the Beatles made a serene song of acceptance called 'Let It Be', the Stones matched this with an offering called 'Let It Bleed', with imagery drawn from someone cutting their wrists. The Stones live in a world of almost surrealist horror, in which at any moment the safe crust of the familiar and the everyday is liable to erupt in a nightmare. Faith is not easily won in their Bosch-like landscape, and when it is it is a triumph, not of hope over experience, but of life reasserting itself within tragedy. Their most moving statement of this, both musically and verbally, comes in a long, narrative song 'You can't always get what you want'. It begins (as do many current songs) in a hymn-like way, in this case with a heavenly choir insisting with soprano purity that you can't always get what you want, but sometimes you get what you need. The mood changes with the softness of the French horn

and Jagger begins to recount the story of an encounter with a
faithless woman.

> I saw her today at the reception
> A glass of wine in her hand
> I knew she was gonna meet her connection
> And her feet was foot-loose, man.

The story continues, until

> I saw her today at the reception
> In her glass was a bleeding man
> She was practised at the art of deception
> Well, I could tell by the blood-stained hand.[10]

Between every verse the message thunders out that you can't
always get what you want, but sometimes you might just find you
get what you need. Gradually this assumes the importance of a
credo, a statement that whatever the appearances to the contrary
there is something meaningful and purposeful about the world,
even in its darkest manifestations. The music picks up speed
until it emerges into a joyful calypso, and then beyond and above
the calypso, blending with its rhythms, we once again hear the
heavenly choir repeating the succinct message that we are indeed
fed, if not always upon the spiritual food of our choice.

Of course, the majority of pop music is not in this class; it is
too frail and ephemeral to carry such insights as these and abounds
in banality of thought and expression, in the crudest kinds of
sexual innuendo, and in the more blatant kinds of commercialism.
It would be foolish to regard pop music in general as soaked in
spirituality. Nevertheless at one point when serious experiment
with acid and with transcendental meditation was changing the
vision of the young, it did make it possible to tell others what
was happening, to record a sudden and shattering encounter
with the Other. What Jung called 'the imperishable world irrupt-
ing into this transitory one'.

A very common expression in pop circles is getting together,
or 'coming together'. 'We'll get it together for you' the pop
group promises its audience, and one of the Beatles' hits was

10 Rolling Stones, 'Let it Bleed' (Decca).

called 'Come Together'. In the obvious physical sense it represents the hope of this generation, a sort of closing of the ranks of
mankind, in which both the obvious kinds of killing, like war, and
the subtler kinds, rejection, condemnation, the withholding of
love and sympathy, become more difficult. On another level it
represents the unifying experience of being 'sent', the ecstatic
moment in which life becomes so meaningful that personal
identity can be surrendered and so mysteriously created at the
same time. And on another level still, it represents the struggling
of the individual towards some kind of wholeness.

> My sweet Lord, I really want to see you
> I really want to be with you
> I really want to see you Lord but it takes
> so long — my Lord.[11]

Pop music, poetry, art have become the distinctive culture
of the Underground, and they imply a rejection of older culture.
Above all they have rejected the culture of words — their poetry
is the weakest of their arts, and words are often used clumsily,
imprecisely, pretentiously, as in this by Joan Baez:

> Only you and I can help the sun rise each coming morning,
> If we don't, it may spend itself out in sorrow,
> You — special, miraculous, unrepeatable, fragile, fearful,
>   tender, lost, sparkling ruby emerald jewel, rainbow
>   splendour person.
> It's up to you.

Words are simply a form of incantation, a way of arousing
emotion without sifting it through the mind, and without the
beat of music to accompany them, they easily become tiresome
and pointless.
   The lack of feeling for words robs the movement of anything
that could be called wit, but wit itself springs from a wryness, even
a cynicism of approach which is foreign to a way of life that is
naive. *Naïveté* must be accompanied by a basic ignorance of the
past and its achievements, and occurs either because people are
genuinely ignorant, or because there is a need to be rid of the

[11] 'All Things Must Pass'.

burdens of the past in order to discover some authentic life and feeling of one's own. Perhaps there are elements of both in the present situation.

Anti-culture has the advantage that it wipes the slate clean and makes all things possible again. There are no wounding standards against which to measure oneself; like a child one paints or writes on, sublimely happy with one's creation. Eventually this gives way to a more self-critical approach (though not before follies have sprouted alongside the masterpieces), but in the meantime those who would never have dared to create anything in a more critical atmosphere have 'done their own thing'.

Anti-culture has the disadvantage, however, that it destroys all basis of cultural judgment, and perhaps this is why a book like Tolkien's *The Lord of the Rings* can be central to the movement, admired, quoted, copied, even lived. The Tolkien *oeuvre* is certainly about journey, in fact about a number of journeys spread over several books. The author is cultured enough himself, with an erudition about European languages and folk-lore that is much in evidence in the books, as the hobbits, dwarfs, goblins, trolls, dragons, and Gandalf the wizard disport themselves. The books are an allegory, a prolonged description of the battle between good and evil, not obviously Christian like C. S. Lewis's Narnia books, yet somehow out of the same stable with their donnish/adolescent humour, and their lack of any sexual relationships. Female characters are virtually non-existent; the hobbits, in particular, seem to get orgastic pleasure out of eating.

The deliberate charm of the story-telling method, the lack of any bite in the humour, the cherubic avuncular cheeriness, together add up to a sentimentality which seems at odds with the freshness and directness of the movement. If they must have a cult, it seems a limited and sterile choice. There are many novelists, less overtly concerned with journey, who have more insight into a situation like the present, though they do not have Tolkien's dangerous gift of simplifying the issues.

With culture deposed it is inevitable that the education system totters too, and the movement is already wanting freer schools, or quite different schools, or a very, very informal method of education that would not be a school as we have known it. School, following Ivan Illich, is seen as part of the brain-washing, conditioning process by which we make a man obedient to society; it is a political rather than a cultural instrument.

This is not a new idea; it has long since been claimed that the 1870 Act which made education compulsory was merely a device to ensure a plentiful supply of clerks for Britain's expanding commercial enterprises, and the sharp way in which children at free schools are sorted into clever and not-so-clever makes it clear that our primary interest is to place future citizens on the assembly belt either to professional or manual work. The Underground will have none of assembly belts and inevitably, therefore, rejects the factories which build them. Perhaps the most far-reaching, because the most obviously attractive, of the movement's ideas will be for a revolution in education. Already vast numbers of the adult and adolescent population are disappointed in the way the education system has dismissed them as unimportant and uninteresting, and might be sympathetic to new methods. The competitiveness, compulsive activity, and passion for status which we firmly instil into children through ordeals like the eleven-plus, are the enemies of everything the Underground stands for. Perhaps they are the enemies of all true culture and civilization.

In the meantime the alternative society subverts the system by mocking at the logical, technological nature of our formal teaching, and at the authoritarian discipline which upholds it. It explores instead lateral thinking, a non-manipulative approach to the world around us, and equality between teacher and taught.

A non-logical approach to life opens the way to many ideas and insights which have long since been dismissed by intelligent people as being superstitious. If the Underground is contemptuous or ignorant of the culture of past generations, it is very knowledgeable about the old wives' tales, and one of the surprises for a student of the movement is to find himself being seriously asked to consider forms of prediction, or beliefs about the body or about food, which he had glibly thought 'science' had demolished years ago.

These are all loosely connected with the idea of religious quest — one asks the *I-Ching* for advice, for example, not so much for material advantage as to learn how to do what one should — and underlying them is the sense that we have collectively lost the path and need not despise ancient ways of finding it again. The multiplicity of these ways is utterly bewildering. No path is too strange, too foreign, too old, or too exacting, for someone somewhere not to want to try it. At this point, it must be said, experimenting goes far beyond those who see themselves as members of the alternative society, and much that follows applies more generally.

People buy sets of yarrow stalks and practise the divination of the *I-Ching*, and sets of Tarot cards with which to tell fortunes. They study the Kabbalah, or the lore about the Third Eye, Tantrism, and Christian mysticism, Zen Buddhism and the Holy Grail. They try astrology and yoga, palmistry and hypnotism, pyramidology and honey cookery. They explore alchemy, druidism, witchcraft, occultism of every sort, Sufism, Shintoism and various kinds of Japanese wisdom. Shops which sell books about such practices, like John Watkins in Cecil Court, London, W.C.2 and the Atlantis shop in Museum Street, enjoy a quiet boom, and whereas their clientele a few years ago might have consisted of middle-aged cranks, together with a solid core of those genuinely curious about the by-ways of spiritual experience, today many of the clients tend to be young and highly intelligent.

Ten or twenty years ago intelligent people might have blushed to tell their friends they had such interests. Now they do so no longer, and either we must conclude that everyone is going mildly dotty, and that in the absence of a strong uniform religion people grasp at anything supernatural, or that through these manifold forms of search, queer as some of them seem, some real attempt at a journey is being made. Is it one journey or many journeys?

A number of people I interviewed made a sharp distinction between witchcraft and other spiritual disciplines, that whereas witchcraft was concerned with trying to obtain control over others, to dominate for one's own purposes, the best of other spiritual disciplines were concerned with a setting free of oneself and others, even if the setting free appeared to demand temporary forms of bondage. Leaving witchcraft on one side, the other spiritual disciplines currently popular while by no means identical often have strong family resemblances. Striking among many of them, and the more striking because it has tended to get left out of traditional Christianity, is the awareness of the importance of the body, of its health, its discipline, its bearing upon the mind and the spirit. Some forms of discipline, in particular hatha yoga,

concentrate upon health, but even so there seems a new awareness that the health of the body opens into a larger landscape
than comfort or beauty or sexual competence. Its followers seem
to have a kind of unspoken hope that it will not just help their
obesity or their constipation, but that it may touch some more
fundamental roots of dissatisfaction. The popularity of it may
indicate intuitive understanding of the deep roots of ill-heath
which are so firmly ignored by modern medicine. It may be too
that there is a kind of poetry about doing movements with names
like the Sun Exercise, the Plough, the Bow, the Cobra, or Sun
and Moon Breathing, which was not to be found in old-fashioned
physical jerks.

Few Westerners have so far been persistent or believing or
brave or foolish enough to want to pass beyond hatha yoga to the
advanced forms of meditative yoga which lie beyond it. Every
now and then one is told of someone who has seriously attempted
to arouse 'Kundalini' the coiled serpent which lies at the base of
the spine just above the anus. Once Kundalini is awakened by
particular techniques he moves up the spine stage by stage, until
he reaches the top of the head and superconsciousness, the
Thousand Petalled Lotus Centre, is achieved. When this happens without supervision from an experienced guru, and it is
alleged that it occurs occasionally in the West, then the result
can easily be insanity.

We seem to prefer journeys with an Eastern flavour. Rider
& Co., a branch of the Hutchinson company which publishes
many books on esoteric subjects, report that their best sales are
in books to do with Buddhism, with the *I-Ching*, with Tarot
(they publish Tarot cards as well as books), and above all in
books of spiritual journey which have an Eastern flavour, such
as Lanza del Vasto's *Return to the Source*. They find that they
can succeed by catering for seekers for whom fine religious distinctions have broken down into a wider concern of what it is to
be a human being in the twentieth century.

Noticeable both in the esoteric bookshops and in the general
approach of Rider & Co., is a respect for the central religious
traditions of mankind — Buddhism, Hinduism, Christianity,
Judaism, Islam.

One way in which religious distinctions have been broken
down has been in the awakening of interest in 'meditation', a

form of spiritual practice not necessarily allied to any particular religion, or even to a belief in God. This acquired popularity when the Beatles at the height of their fame took it up and travelled to India to pursue their interest, but many have continued quietly working at it since, feeling that it counteracts the pressures of our active society. One of the many places where people go to learn about meditation is the School of Meditation, a non profit-making organisation with headquarters at Holland Park in London. Students come to the headquarters, a simply but beautifully furnished house in London, with plain colours and lines, and 'Japanese' flower arrangements. The house has no regular staff — those who have undergone the training in meditation in time go on to undertake training others.

The School is Vedic in inspiration, deriving its teaching from the Upanishads and the Bhagavad-Gita. It does not seem eager to retain its Eastern image, however, now that many of its students and teachers are English, and the quotations in its advertising material tend to be from European writers.

The School thinks of its training as practical in nature, in helping people to discover a technique which will enable them to achieve greater self-realisation. The object of such a technique and such a self-realisation is to return to the sense of unity already experienced earlier in life and then lost.

What the School tries to offer is a system and knowledge. It teaches people to focus their attention inwards in a particular way, so that even if they are in an agitated state they can still achieve the necessary concentration. They are told that this cannot be done by effort, but rather by the giving up of effort, and a return to a natural state. The end-result appears to be attaining an awareness rather like that of a baby; it means resting in one's own condition, which in turn is supposed to lead to a confidence in being oneself. People undertaking a course of meditation often find that they become far less tired and are much better able to do their daily job; they can concentrate on the work in hand and not wear themselves out with fruitless speculation.

Those who decide to take the course are received with a simple quasi-religious Indian ceremony which often makes a great appeal to them. They bring the traditional gift to the teacher of fruit, flowers and white linen, e.g. a handkerchief, and are asked to make a donation to the School of one week's net income. (This is to keep the way open for others who wish to make use of the School in the future.)

They are then taught a technique of meditation in an exact and precise form and they go away from the room, find a quiet spot in the School either on a chair or on the floor and begin to practise it at once. They are instructed to practise it at home twice a day, morning and evening for fifteen to thirty minutes at a time, and they return to the School twice during the first week for their progress to be checked. Thereafter there are probably weekly visits in keeping with the needs and wishes of the pupil. Several months later, for those who wish it, there is the option of teaching by an Indian teacher in which spiritual truths (of all religions) are expounded.

It sounds a fairly unadventurous spiritual route, or perhaps unambitious is more the word. No wild talk of union with God, no short cuts by drugs, no very exacting regime, but on the contrary the promise that it is perfectly possible to do a normal job and do it all the better while daily practising meditation. Nothing anarchic about the Maharishi's followers; if they were to change society they would clearly do it from within, contributing their quietened nerves, their meditative perspective, their renewed sense of their own value to a frenetic society while holding down nine-to-five jobs. Not necessarily the worse for that.

But perhaps this is to ignore the many different kinds of people who take up the School's technique and mould it to their own needs and characteristics. Their pupils, they claim, come from the greatest range imaginable of age, background and intelligence.

It is clear that one of the attractions of the School is that as soon as a pupil has fully mastered the meditative technique he is required to help and instruct others; this 'pupil-teacher' relationship simultaneously satisfies the desire to instruct and to be instructed.

The School's credo is set out carefully in their introductory booklet (fine Roman lettering on the cover, lots of white spaces between bits of text).

The desire to know and be oneself fully and completely lies behind all our activities, manifesting as an ever-changing desire first for one thing, and then for another.

But there is no lasting satisfaction in pursuing small and temporary desires. For it is a law that the small cannot satisfy the large. The Self needs satisfaction in accordance with its own size and performance. Lasting satisfaction comes only through realising the completeness of Self, the creative principle which lives in the hearts of all.

Through meditation discover Self and so uncover the first cause and upholder of life, the true nature of man.

Those who are in search of a more dramatic religious approach than this, particularly the very young, turn to the Radha Krishna Temple in Bury Place. The followers of this cult can be seen daily in the streets of the West End of London singing the Hare Krishna mantra. They wear yellow robes, the girls with long hair, the boys with their heads shaved but with one long plait growing from the back of their heads. They play drums, cymbals, wind instruments. Sometimes one of them is seen alone sitting meditating cross-legged in a public place such as the forecourt of the British Museum.

On several evenings a week they hold services at their temple, slow chanting gradually giving way to increasing excitement and activity. Keen students of Hare Krishna describe the extraordinary, unforgettable beauty of this event when it goes well, a group experience that reaches and delights all whom it touches. But like all group experiences it cannot be guaranteed to work, and when it doesn't it can be pathetic and embarrassing. Excitement cannot be produced as a matter of will, and even techniques of chanting, drumming, and movement, though effective, are not infallible.

The Radha Krishna people are strict in their discipline — no drink or drugs, and a vegetarian diet. Sex is also rigidly controlled, and the young followers are expected to be chaste. Ecstasy is permitted, therefore, only through the channel of the singing and dancing.

If some forms of search take the form of joining bodies of believers, or anyhow practisers, as in the case of the School of Meditation, for many more it seems to take the form of a craze for prediction. A purely rational approach to life finds it hard to explain prediction, and indeed is scornful of the possibility, but it is this which makes the interest in it so significant; it implies a rejection of the idea that a purely rationalistic explanation of man's experiences is 'enough', and a rejection of the scientific, technological culture in which recent generations have been brought up.

But why should rejection of the scientific culture take the form of trying to read the future? Partly, no doubt, because of profound fears about what the future will bring, but also perhaps because prediction — horoscopes, reading the auspices, telling fortunes, etc., has been so profoundly out of fashion, because of scientific and cultural influences, that it was due for a return to popularity. Or is there a deeper reason, an intuition, or at least a hope, that all life is one, that the future and the past are bound together in some purposive way that is more than simple causality?

Some forms of prediction, such as palmistry, have no particular interest in man's spiritual journey — they claim only to tell him what will happen to him, and do not seem to have any very developed theory about the way this prediction may itself determine the course of events. Others, such as *The Book of Change*, the *I-Ching*, are principally interested in what a man ought to do. By 'ought' they mean not so much what actions are socially responsible (as we tend to do in the West when we say someone 'ought' to do something), as what actions help to make the individual the man of knowledge, or the man of virtue — the Superior Man, as some translations put it — who will not even want to commit crimes, which, in the eyes of the Chinese who composed the book, stem from a basic ignorance about the kind of world it is.

The *I-Ching* is about Change, the change which man both dreads and longs for, would like to control, but is often forced simply to accept. 'Change', remarks one of the book's recent editors, John Blofeld, 'which is never-ending, proceeds according to certain universal and observable rules. In relying upon the *I-Ching* to reveal the future, we are not dealing with magic but calculating the general trend of events and seeking the best way to accord with that trend by relating whatever matter we have in mind to the predictable cycle (or cycles) of events to which it belongs.'[12]

In other words it is not interested in trying to control events

[12] John Blofeld, *The Book of Change* (Allen & Unwin, 1968).

but in helping man to understand his relations to the world about him, and to harmonise with it, one of the roles which religion has played in the West.

Like the Bible the *I-Ching* is an exceedingly ancient book, the work of a number of hands though much more unified in style. Similarly it has been used by pious (and impious) men for centuries as a source of study, a guide to conduct, and a kind of arbiter of how social affairs should be conducted. (Mr. Blofeld has a theory that the movements of the Chinese army along the Indian frontier in 1962–3 possessed characteristics reminiscent of the strategic methods of *The Book of Change*.) It is a garnering of centuries of human experience, and those who are capable of imagining 'inspiration' as something more than the imagination and insights of the wisest men would probably want to claim that it is 'inspired' in the way that this is also claimed about the Bible. What it provides is profound spiritual insights in the form of a horoscope.

The method of divination is to formulate a question which one wishes to ask and then to sit down with a set of fifty sticks, traditionally yarrow stalks. (There is a much simpler and quicker method of doing the whole calculation with coins.) Traditionally there is a bowing and incense lighting ritual which precedes the divination, but I doubt if many Westerners practise this. One of the fifty sticks is removed, and the remaining forty-nine are tossed on the table with the right hand. Then with a series of throws and dividing up of sticks numbers are arrived at which supply the first line of a hexagram. The whole process is then repeated another five times until all six lines are achieved, and these will be either *yin* (broken) or *yang* (unbroken) lines. Whatever design of *yin* and *yang* lines results is looked up in a table of hexagrams, and the appropriate one is then consulted. Each hexagram has a name, an image, and an oracle. Those who are most expert in the interpretation of the *I-Ching* claim to be able to tell the oracle just by considering the image (the images are natural objects — fire, a mountain, a pool, etc., though they also have secondary meanings), but the oracle is there in the book to be consulted. The text also gives comments upon the different lines of the hexagram and their meaning.

What no one text of a hexagram can reveal adequately is the view of man and his life which the *I-Ching* puts forward. It undoubtedly sees him upon a journey, in which his attempt is always to behave as 'the Superior Man'. The Superior Man cares passionately about virtue, which he sees in a more situational way than men have in the West, as the correct response to circumstances. He is not ashamed of ambition, either for fame or prosperity, as the 'good man' in the West has tended to be, yet he is urged continually by the book to set his personal longings within a wider context, which includes the needs of 'the people'. And he is encouraged to realise that to be human implies constant exposure to the ebb and flow of good fortune, and this must be accepted rather than struggled against. 'Loss and gain, filling and emptying — each occurs at the proper time', as the book says. The real danger is a kind of self-will, which allows one to lose the necessary harmony with one's surroundings. 'When it is time to stop, then stop; when the time comes for action, then act! By choosing activity and stillness, each at the proper time, a man achieves glorious progress.'

The book has a calm approach to man's sensual needs. 'If the loins are stilled', it warns in one hexagram, 'the heart will suffocate', but as with all else it seeks a sense of proportion. In a line which indicates 'sensation in the thighs', it makes the pithy comment, 'He cleaves so closely to his wife (handmaiden, etc.), that for him to continue in this manner would be shameful.'

The book's favourite expression concerns 'righteous persistence'. 'Righteous persistence brings reward', it says over and over again, and with the help of the oracle man is expected to discover the course of righteousness encouraged by a great deal of poetic imagery, much of it with an ironic note which makes it more piquant.

'The well has been cleaned out; to my heart's sorrow, no one drinks from it.'

'The prince's food is overturned and his person soiled — misfortune.'

'After the thunderstorm, the paths are muddy.'

'The lame can walk . . . the one-eyed man can see.'

Yet despite all the complications of the hexagrams and the yarrow stalks, how does consulting the *I-Ching* differ from the well-established, though now largely discontinued, habit of using the Bible as an oracle, opening it at random, and using whatever passage the eye fell on as an answer to a question? The *I-Ching* itself, after all, or rather the method of divination derived from it, is an assertion that there is no such thing as randomness, since the very way that one throws the sticks (and even probably the mistakes that one makes in the throwing and the calculation; it is a muddling business) is thought to determine an important answer. So that there seems no reason that one's opening of the Bible, or turning of its pages, might not be equally 'meant'.

It is difficult to draw any distinction save one between the old practice of bibliomancy and the new one (in the West, that is) of consulting the *I-Ching*. This derives from the disparate literary styles of the Bible and the *I-Ching*. The Bible, in addition to its passages of moral exhortation such as Proverbs, or the Sermon on the Mount, contains enormous sections of narrative, as well as long sections of ritual legalism. In places, particularly perhaps the parables of the New Testament, exclamatory passages in the Psalms, and other poetic sections of prophecy, it has strong parallels with the *I-Ching*, but on the whole what distinguishes it is a much more positive content; it tends, in intention at least, to be unambiguous, and about a particular historical situation.

The *I-Ching*, on the other hand, like the famous Taoist classic *The Tao te Ching* to which it has a strong resemblance, has a kind of boundarylessness about it. Its passages can mean anything or nothing, and this is due not to any literary failure to communicate meaning, but rather a deep conviction that life is ambiguous, and that virtue, power, prosperity, brotherly love, are not always quite what they appear at first glance. Man is beset by contradictions, and the quickest path to any goal is not necessarily the shortest line between two points.

It is, perhaps the boundarylessness of the *I-Ching* which makes it effective. The supplicant receives the strange, shapeless reply with the expectancy of someone who has just asked a question and who has undergone a complicated anticipatory procedure (it can take half an hour). The result is a focusing of attention which makes for peculiar sensitivity to the answer.

There is a wealth of lore among Western devotees of the *I-Ching* about people who, mistrusting their first answer, threw the sticks once or twice more and got the same reply. Or of those who used the book frivolously or for some 'impure' motive such as gambling, and got a very dusty answer for their pains.

The book has some crushing comments to deliver, as for instance
'Watching through door-cracks is of advantage to women. Nevertheless it is also shameful', or 'Trifling with unimportant matters, the traveller draws upon himself calamity'.

Many who use the book in the West, and who try to keep their
'scientific' wits about them, are struck by the extent that asking
the book comes to feel like asking a person, a person for whose
insight and ability to see through their pretentions and defences
(yet with a certain delicacy and gentleness) they have a growing
respect. They find it hard to remember that it is only an 'ordinary' book they are referring to.

Yet the 'boundarylessness' of the book might be thought to
offer a key to a rational explanation, at least for those prepared
to accept psychoanalytic insights. The book, like any work of
art, is full of profound symbolism — fire, water, wind, etc. When
the concentration is focused upon these symbols, each of them
meaningful to the unconscious, then it may become possible to
understand happenings in the conscious life in a different way and
at a different level. In some ways the process is rather like the
interpretation of a dream which takes place in psychoanalysis.
The analyst offers various interpretations of the dream-
material, and accepts one or more of them, possibly adding
interpretations of his own, and uses the interpretations as a kind
of window into his unconscious processes. Of course, the 'given'
in the case of the analytic situation is the dream which the patient
has spontaneously produced, and the 'given' in the case of the
I-Ching is only the conscious question (the commentary of the
hexagram serving the function of the analyst's interpretation).

In both cases, though, we are exercising a kind of 'meditative'
function, a function otherwise used in prayer, or in the course of
some aesthetic experiences. It is the quality of the symbols it
employs which seems to me to make the consultation of the
I-Ching a very different thing from consulting a newspaper
horoscope.

There are thus two kinds of explanation of the way the I-Ching
works, one of them depending upon a 'harmonious' view of the
universe, the other upon a particular view of how the human
mind works. The two are not mutually exclusive, though one
can believe either without believing the other.

Another kind of divination which is attended by some of the

same awe as surrounded the *I-Ching*, is fortune-telling with the Tarot pack. Readers of T. S. Eliot, or of Charles Williams, are aware of certain names associated with the Tarot — the 'Hanged Man', for example, or the 'Greater Trumps'. Many of the names have a poetic appeal — 'The Hierophant', 'The Lovers', 'The Hermit', 'The Wheel of Fortune', 'The Empress', 'The Fool', 'The Magician', The Knight of Pentacles', 'The King of Swords', 'The Page of Cups', The Queen of Wands', and since most of the packs of cards on sale are reprinted from old designs there is something archaic and haunting about the pictures on the cards.

The origin of the cards is lost in history, but there is a theory that, like the gypsies who have so often used them, they come from Egypt. There are seventy-eight cards in the Tarot pack, fifty-six of them in four suits, the ancestors of the modern pack of playing cards, known as the Minor Arcana, and twenty-two additional cards, known at the Major Arcana.

Of the four suits, Wands, Cups, Swords and Pentacles, Wands were eventually to become Clubs, Cups to become Hearts, Swords to become Spades and Pentacles to become Diamonds. Wands, according to Eden Gray in *The Tarot Revealed* are associated with enterprise and glory, Cups with love and happiness, Swords with strife and misfortune and Pentacles with money. There are the usual fourteen cards in each suit, ten numbered from Ace to Ten, and four Court cards — King, Queen, Knight and Page. 'The King often symbolises the Spirit; the Queen, the Soul; the Knight, the Ego; and the Page, the Body.'

The Major Arcana, according to Gray, represent a sort of shorthand of metaphysics and mysticism. The symbol on each card 'represents a distinct principle, law, power or element in Nature. The designs on the cards also illuminate the life of man, his joys and sorrows, hopes and despairs. They further indicate his search for the wisdom which enables him to control his passions and help in his transition to . . . spheres, where he enters into the things of the spirit.' The Major Arcana has threatening aspects. It includes the figure of Death, a horseman in some packs, in others a skeleton holding a scythe, the person of the Devil, the Sun, the Moon, and the World.

Such symbols as these easily lead on into meditative processes, and it is interesting that whereas the symbols as *ideas* are traditional and unchanging, the actual illustrations are not. How they are represented is not all that important; it is enough to remind the seeker of what the card stands for and he can finish the task with his own imagination, helped to a greater or lesser degree by the power of the artist who designed the cards. This may be because the symbols of the Major Arcana are already familiar to him, either because the Devil, Death, the Sun, the Hermit, the Fool, etc., are part of the common heritage in which he has been brought up, or because they are part of the intimate furniture of his own mind, or, most probably, both of these things. The Jungians would call such symbols 'archetypal', nuclei of power and numinosity which have both an individual and a collective importance.

Any one of these cards might, it would be supposed, yield material for profound meditation, but in fact the Tarot divination works by the combination of cards used in the fortune-telling. These 'add up' to a particular result, a predominance of Swords, for instance, suggesting conflict or striving, or a predominance of Pentacles suggesting prosperity. There are a number of methods by which the Tarot cards are read.

Experiments with the Tarot cards are reminiscent of experiments with the I-Ching. The profundity of the symbols makes them of universal interest — no potential reader of the cards is likely to remain unmoved by the chances of love, prosperity, ambition, conflict and growth. The number of cards turned, however, each with a fairly distinct meaning which can be looked up in text-books of Tarot, means that the Tarot makes many more statements about the situation than the I-Ching does and moreover ties them firmly to the past, the future, and to cerain circumscribed areas, such as one's fears, or the opinion of others. It is, therefore, not only easier to show that it is right or wrong, but easy to feel that it is contradicting itself in a rather muddling and irritating way. Given contradictory readings it becomes necessary to select which cards to give predominance to, and it is a temptation to err on the optimistic side, to note the hints of prosperity and love rather than of loneliness, sickness or failure. Of course, it may be that just as the I-Ching reminds one that life is a continual process of change, of filling and emptying, so the contradictory Tarot cards state, what is no more than the truth for most of us, that life is a mixture of joy and disappointment, of success and failure. What is missing is the poetry of the *I-Ching*, the deep insights into human folly and the gentleness and humour with which these are expressed. The Tarot interpretations are modern and usually in fairly pedestrian English, and the brutality with which they are expressed in the books (though not by those who are skilled in handling the cards) is rather painful. 'Voided ambition, unethical application of skill. . . . Inertia, stagnation. A young man of careless habit. . . . Duties neglected, dependence on others. . . .'

The value of the Tarot cannot lie in the words but in the pictures, and perhaps it is because Western culture is gradually losing its verbal emphasis and is coming to value non-verbal means of communication that these cards with their ancient symbols have begun to speak to people again. Having almost lost sight of traditional insights like the close connection between birth and death, insights built alike into Christianity and into the natural life with which we are surrounded, we suddenly rediscover them again in the Tarot, where turning up the card 'Death' may mean 'Transformation . . . destruction followed or preceded by transformation. The change may be in the form of consciousness. Sometimes it may mean birth and renewal.'

The taste for prediction also follows less spiritual paths than this, of course. Newspaper horoscopes are exceedingly popular, but unlike the *I-Ching* or the Tarot they offer no traditional wisdom, and do not attempt to depict the 'emptying' and 'filling' process and the natural philosophy which underlies such a point of view. Instead, they concentrate mainly on cheerful items (there is rarely any mention of illness, accident or catastrophe, and it is doubtful if editors would publish them if there were), and seem to exercise a comforting function, a sort of dummy amid the perils and fears of life.

It would be a mistake, however, to suppose that the current craze for astrological prediction represented no more than the easy comfort of the newspaper horoscope. The Astrological Association, a body with 800 members, whose numbers have grown quickly in the past three years' conducts its affairs in very much the sort of intelligent, sober way that any professional body (as it might be of lawyers, psycho-analysts, architects) conducts theirs, with an annual conference at Fitzwilliam College, Cambridge, and an obvious wish to relate its own body of learning to scientific thinking of the day. Unlike

the lawyers or the architects, but rather more like the psycho-
analysts, it is not entirely confident of its public standing, and
several articles in its magazine *The Astrological Journal* suggest the frustration of those who have something they want to
share with others who spurn the offer.

> Most astrologers would rejoice if a general knowledge of the
> science and art (i.e. astrology) could be attained by all who have
> a reasonable standard of rational and non-rational education.
> Indeed, perhaps the day is not all that far away when birth
> charts will be displayed in classes, offices, workshops and all
> places where people of goodwill spend time in community.
> Could this not be a vital part of the Aquarian brotherhood
> of man, this getting below the surface to evaluate from cosmic
> symbolism to universal profundities, our fellow being with
> whom . . . we have to live, work and converse. Might we not
> all gain in tolerance, compassion and insight from such mutual
> understanding? Or . . . would we form prejudices against
> our fellow men, based entirely on our own interpretations of
> the contents of their charts?

This confident, unfanatical approach seems typical of the
Association, and the confidence is born of the speed with which
their numbers have increased. They now have a Faculty of
Astrological Studies which runs a correspondence course and sets
an examination for which a Diploma is given. Their member-
ship consists of about sixty per cent women and forty per cent
men, most of them middle-aged. The Association so far does not
attract young people, not even the astrologers of the 'Gandalf's
Garden' school, whose interest in the subject is perhaps more
poetic than that of the Association. The Association do not see
a man's chart as in any way controlling what happens to him in
his life, but rather as revealing his 'raw temperament' on which
other things such as his heredity and environment have also
worked. They are eager for controlled experiments to show that
a correctly drawn chart can provide information that is both
accurate and useful. *The Astrological Journal* carries many
articles discussing the way that man is 'geared-in' to a 'meaningful solar system pattern', and the Spring 1972 issue includes
among other things an attempt to understand the astrological con-

junctions relating to murderers or to murder victims, to neurosis and psychosis, as well as to genius in various forms. One article, by Ingrid Lind, the Vice-President of the Association, gives a lengthy assessment of the chart of a child, Andrew, which goes into elaborate detail about the temperament he will have, the sort of work he will enjoy, the weaknesses of his character and his difficulties in getting along with other people. Also, it mentions conjunctions of planets which accompanied two serious shocks in the child's life — an accident in which he was nearly blinded, and the separation and divorce of his parents. The general tone of the study is an unfatalistic one; it does not regard the subject as helpless in the face of his temperament, but rather as one in a position to protect himself against particular dangers — a coldness towards others, a tendency to bore, an unwillingness to serve an apprenticeship.

It is not easy for those educated in a casual or 'scientific' view of the world to make any sense of this kind of thinking. Like the Emperor with the new clothes, we feel we are in danger of being taken in. The trouble is that we do not have any training to enable us to distinguish possible truth from possible nonsense in a field like astrology. It is clear that it does not fit into the 'billiard ball' view life, i.e. A causes B, B causes C, and we do not have any other developed intellectual approach which would make us feel confident in distinguishing the genuine from the bogus, or even any definition of what 'genuine' might mean in this context. We are left only with intuition, a notoriously dangerous guide, a hunch that there may be things which 'work' which do not operate in a causal way.

The popular interest in prediction, and especially in astrological prediction makes the question more acute. Does it represent yet another example of pathetic human credulity, the determination of the masses to be gulled, no matter how educators strive to inform and enlighten them? Or are we witnessing a kind of mass intuition, an awareness that causality is not enough, and that we have to look behind and beneath this to do justice to the kind of world it is?

If that is what it is there are those who do not hesitate to take commercial advantage of it. One publisher, Purnell, owned by B.P.C. Publishing, has brought out 'an encyclopaedia of the supernatural' called *Man, Myth and Magic* in 112 weekly instalments.

The first instalment had a hideous mask — of witch, or devil — on the front, and beneath it the legend *The Most Unusual Magazine ever published*. The instalments are lavishly and beautifully illustrated with colour reproductions of innumerable famous pictures, drawings and woodcuts. The first full page colour picture was of a misty, mysterious forest, and over the page the mummified corpse of Rameses II, withered flesh upon protruding bones. Subsequent pictures included the tormenting of St. Anthony, the picture of a naked sorceress on a broomstick, Japanese, Indian, Aztec and medieval European paintings, and an engraving from Foxe's *Book of Martyrs* with detailed pictures of the types of torture used by the Inquisition. There is a strong emphasis on physical suffering in this instalment of the encyclopaedia. Apart from St. Anthony and the Inquisition there are pictures of people being broken on the wheel, having hair and teeth pulled out as part of martyrdom, being burned as witches, subjected to African initiation rites, and beaten to cure mental illness, and there are also detailed verbal descriptions of various kinds of savage torture.

The strongest interest in the magazine seems to be in witchcraft, with lengthy descriptions of the 'Aberdeen witches', of the 'possession' by the nuns of Aix-en-Provence, and a number of old woodcuts of witchcraft, including one of women kissing the Devil's anus.

There is a careful exposition of the hero myth, rather finely illustrated by a vase painting of Superman, a picture of Superman, and the Uccello painting of St. George killing the dragon.

The encyclopaedia has a highly respectable editorial board, including Dr. Glyn Daniel, Professor E. R. Dodds, Mircea Eliade, Dr. William Sargant,, and Professor Zaehner. The editor is Richard Cavendish, according to the magazine a 'leading authority on magic and witchcraft' who has published a book called *The Black Arts*.

What the encyclopaedia has set out to do is to undertake a course of popular education in the field of myth, and in the process it seems to lean rather heavily towards sensation, in the form of religion, witchcraft, demonology, sickness, madness, and cruelty. Much of the material used, particularly the illustrations, would seem open to the charge of attempting to titillate quite as much as to instruct.

Much of its appeal is of a 'gosh-golly' kind. 'At last it is possible to bring discussion of the supernatural out of the dark — a privilege denied even to our parents . . .' But alongside this claim to enlighten is the hint of endowing readers with mystic powers. 'The question of magic', the encyclopaedia says, quoting from a source it doesn't reveal, 'is a question of discovering and employing hitherto unknown forces in Nature.' What this appears to play upon is not just the credulity of simple and ill-educated people who long to be able to assert themselves more effectively, but also the unresolved bewilderment which troubles modern men, forbidden superstition, yet still feeling himself individually helpless in a difficult and frightening world.

'Every time you cross your fingers, say a prayer, or read your "stars" in the paper, you express your surviving belief in the supernatural. This is a unique opportunity to make up your mind on this vital area of human experience', says *Man, Myth and Magic*, and out of this conflict excellent sales were made — they had soared to 75,000 a week within a year, with the prospect of American sales five times that figure.

The seventies' journey, with its openness to new (and old) ideas also opens itself to silliness and to the exploitation of silliness. We cannot explore some of the ideas which seem promising without temporarily abandoning some kinds of intellectual rigour, but there is peril in the exercise, not least the peril of coming to despise the intellect and its disciplines. Some return to *naïveté* seems inevitable if we are to ask once again the questions which we thought we had stopped asking, yet *naïveté* leaves us defenceless by useful weapons such as ridicule and satire. The breakdown of conventional religion over a period of several generations had made us religiously illiterate — few 'well-educated' people alive today who are not clergymen have much real grasp of theology or what the Christian doctrines are about — and this in itself forces *naïveté* upon us willy-nilly.

The sorts of religion so far discussed have ignored the role of the Churches and of Christianity in the present search for 'journey'. The church-going community, with important exceptions, has little use for the more esoteric forms of religious expression so far discussed, and the alternative, anarchic, or pop society has little use for established religion. Not that it is hostile to it, or even embarrassed by it, as the older generation are still apt to be by religious discussion. God seems a natural interest to the alternative society, together with meditative and contemplative disciplines, and group 'experiences' of one kind and another which seem relevant to a religious search. What is an open question, however, is the bearing these disciplines have on ethical conduct. Revolt against the Christian sexual ethic which is also revolt against the society of their parents, is central to the beliefs of the alternative society, and it is in this area perhaps that they are having the greatest influence on society as a whole, challenging ideas — about the family, marriage, fidelity, homosexuality — which once appeared unchallengeable. It seems possible, too, that Eastern ways of thought are already gaining ground on the authoritarianism of Christianity, with its hard and fast view of good and evil, insisting that more flexibility is needed in human conduct. The Eastern view is that right has more to do with conformity to a certain harmony in the world about one (failure to do so being due rather to ignorance than to wickedness) than obedience to set rules.

The history of Christianity since the war (in all its larger manifestations) does not suggest fossilisation, in fact it would be possible to argue that the Churches have tried harder than any political body to reorganise their structures along more workable lines, and to reappraise their function in the community. There has been a hurricane of reform on the one hand, and an earthquake of radical questioning on the other.

The Roman Catholic Church has courageously struggled, ever since the Second Vatican Council, with the attempt to replace a paternalistic structure with a more democratic, consultative one. It has transformed its liturgy, its religious orders, the training of its priesthood, and in some countries has allied itself with left-wing movements whose aim is to bring about social justice, with or without violence.

The Churches in this country have stream-lined their administrative machinery, and have set on foot innumerable imaginative schemes both to make Christianity relevant to a new generation, and to meet the particular social needs of post-war society. New church buildings, house churches, shorter and livelier services, skilful use of drama, music and art, the use of modern translations of the Bible, week-end courses, have all played an important part in the teaching of the Churches. In their social roles the Churches have operated schemes to build a sense of community on new estates, have pioneered and run advisory and counselling services, and housing trusts, and schemes to help human beings in every kind of trouble and difficulty — divorcees, homosexuals, alcoholics, tramps, mentally handicapped, mentally ill, and those in the Third World.

Some groups of Christians have gone beyond this kind of direct service to their fellow-men, seeing their contribution rather as one of changing the political structure and altering the very basis of the society in which so many wounds are inflicted and injustices occur. They have used their energies for political demonstration and for work within parties dedicated to radical, or revolutionary change, or within groups who see anarchy as our first and best hope.

On the whole though it must be said that in England Christianity is not taking a revolutionary form, and that those who still go to church are middle-class and not particularly ashamed of it. Last year I attended a 'School of Prayer' being held at a very large, popular church near the Notting Hill area, with a large congregation of young people, many of them students. Since this church is, geographically, in the heart of the Underground country, I wondered whether any hippy influences might have penetrated the congregation, but dress, hair-style and ideas were all strikingly conventional, and when moral questions were raised (as they often seemed to be) they were based on a traditional and conventional approach to sexuality.

Did the church repel the unconventional and anarchistic members of the community because of its tradition, or was it that it did not change because only the 'respectable' young came to it? Was it the young who did come who forced the church into a particular rigid mould, because they felt safer within an unchanging and unchangeable framework?

For there is no doubt that the area in which the Church has been slowest to change has been sexuality. Most other change has been welcomed gladly and courageously, but it would still take a rash bishop to say publicly that pre-marital sex might be a good thing, that some kinds of marriage make adultery almost inevitable, or that sexual intercourse between homosexuals is not a sin. This is not, I think, because there is not acute awareness in the Church of the kinds of hypocrisy which traditional sexual morality encouraged. Clergy are recipients of enough confidences about unhappy marriage, sexual frustration, and deviation to question the efficacy of traditional teaching. So that it is a puzzle that however rigorous the questioning in other areas of thought (even ones fundamental to the continuance of the Church like the existence of God, or the historicity of Christ) it tends to trail away when sexuality is mentioned. In this area there virtually *is* no debate, and when the organisers of an event like the 'Festival of Light' claim to be speaking for 'Christians' in upholding the moral standards of this country against corruption, there are few Christian voices raised to say that this is not how they see the situation at all.

Might this be because while the Churches tend to appear as patriarchies, with male dignitaries, and an all-male priesthood (with important exceptions in the Free Churches), the real power in them is often wielded by middle-aged, middle-class women, largely because of numerical superiority and freedom either from doing a job or caring for a young family? Middle-aged women tend to feel vulnerable to discussion which questions the viability of the family, the demand of absolute faithfulness in marriage, and the demand of absolute continence in the young. Despite considerable pressure from the clergy the Mothers' Union has not felt able to admit divorced women to its ranks feeling that this would strike at the 'sanctity of marriage'.

This attitude of certainty, and of being 'above' the debate, at a time when everyone else is seeking, questioning, wondering, about the importance of sexuality and how this can best be expressed, means that the Church is automatically at one side of the present debate. Those who are sure they have all the answers are boring know-alls to those who determine to reach some first-hand understanding of a situation.

On the other hand, there is within Christian circles a residual interest in and knowledge of contemplative techniques, and there are a very few people left — usually in contemplative orders — who are part of the continuous Christian tradition of contemplative prayer. Amid so much blind experiment, they represent, as do the Buddhist teachers, a body of people who have had experience of transcendental states, and are not particularly surprised by anything that happens in them. This gives them an influence out of all proportion to their numbers. In such Christian circles there is often an interest in and a knowledge of Eastern techniques, which derived originally perhaps from the studies in Zen made by the American Cistercian, Thomas Merton.

So far as religious orders are concerned the contemplative ones have survived rather better than the active ones so far in terms of finding recruits or 'vocations'. It is indeed easier to establish a rationale for the one than the other, since it is difficult to understand why one must join a religious order in order to teach or nurse (the answer that you will do the job better being rather insulting to those who take up these professions without joining a religious order), but rather easier to see why, if you want to spend much of your life in prayer, a way of life which supports you in doing this may seem a good idea.

The contemplative orders often seem rather better than other Christians in establishing links with those who have no faith or who have a faith which owes little to Christian orthodoxy. This is partly perhaps because people sometimes turn to religious communities when in a state of despair over their present way of life. In physical or mental crisis, in marital conflict or beset with desperate worries about work, money, or health, people are more open to the concerns of the contemplative. Possibly those who enter the stricter orders are themselves extreme personalities and this may make them especially sensitive to extreme situations of all kinds. Again, it must be said that there are certain technical and psychological problems common to all who seriously embark upon exercises of prayer, meditation, contemplation, or whatever it is called, and though one feels repugnance in saying it, people do take a human pleasure in exchanging experiences and problems on this sort of level. This may mean that the contemplative can make immediate contact with a hippy, or a psychoanalyst, a Buddhist, a Vedantist, while finding it hard to have more than a superficial conversation with a fellow-Christian who has only the most formal conception of prayer.

Finally, and most important, it would seem that the contemplatives are particularly sensitive to the spirit of the times, entering at a deep level into what people's deepest needs and longings are and so being able to respond swiftly and accurately when approached by those who do not, to all appearances, speak their particular language. There is a paradoxical sense in which enclosed communities in particular seem to live much more 'in the world' than do most Christians; there is something dark and perilous about the contemplative experience which makes it hard to forget that one is a human being before all else, constantly endangered, and often alone. The experience of solitude throws up apparitions, phantasms, temptations, ecstasies which make it impossible to ignore either the joy or the pain of being human. And the nearness to madness, which much current thinking and behaviour is bent on ignoring or denying, is well understood.

There have been some valiant attempts within the Churches to encourage Christians to look more deeply at their inner problems, and particularly their problems of relationship. Some notable experiments in group dynamics have been carried out on an inter-denominational basis by the Church of England Board of Education, some with monks and nuns, some with priests and lay people. Other bodies, such as the Richmond Fellowship, have also undertaken group dynamics with mainly Christian groups, discovering, perhaps predictably, that the most difficult thing, for priests in particular, was not to be in a 'helping' (and so superior) capacity, but to accept a need for help and wisdom from others.

One of the most vigorous Christian movements in the last few years has been Pentecostalism, presumably because it answers the desperate hunger to experience instead of merely to mouth religious truths. The Dominicans at Oxford decided a few years ago that they would like to establish contact with the Pentecostalists, and they invited a local pastor to come and discuss his beliefs with them. This meeting was not a success — 'we found his theology either incomprehensible or repugnant' — but in spite of this initial setback some of them began to go regularly to Pentecostalist prayer meetings. The spirit of these meetings — the total lack of religious inhibition — gradually gripped them until the meetings became the high spot of the week, and they felt some of the religious fervour was being carried back to their own, intensely formal, prayers in choir. Is it significant that it should be the Dominicans, probably the most cerebral of all religious orders, who felt a need to seek out a form of Christianity which relies almost entirely upon emotion at the expense of a coherent intellectual basis of theology?

Apart from the search for ecstasy, and some more realistic assessment of its future role as only one guide among many, what lies before formal Christianity in the immediate future? I believe that the biggest battle will come over the person of Christ. The battle lines are already forming between those to whom Christ is the great cult figure, who must be experienced in some vaguely defined way before any kind of wholeness can be achieved, and those for whom the historical Christ is of limited interest, and the cult-figure even less so, but who find the archetype of Christ meaningful in their attempt to understand their own life and those of others. For the latter group Christ is the human experience in section, a kind of focus by which it is possible to make sense of vocation, transfiguration, crucifixion and resurrection as each man struggles with these experiences inside himself.

Any cult of Jesus which is principally interested in his historicity, or in seeing him as an example to be emulated, or as a kind of touchstone by which to judge the authenticity of others, is at war with this latter insight for which the Christ-experience is essentially one to be discovered within the person (and within his relations with others) without pressure or manipulation by others.

CHAPTER SIX

The Coming Journey

THE HERO EMERGES FROM HIS RELATIVELY OBSCURE
background — related as he is to kings and princes — and sets
forth to conquer the monster. He is marked with the loneliness of
the orphan, but against this he sets either his overwhelming ambition, or a sense of vocation which will not allow him to rest in
his humble home. His infancy has been marked by signs and
portents which let him know that he was no ordinary child, and
he has cherished these, and cherished them all the more in the
isolation from other children which has often been his lot.

He has unusual powers, whether of strength or intelligence or
insight, and he may also have powerful and supernatural friends,
perhaps magicians or gods. Before he embarks on his fateful
journey, quest, or voyage, he has a number of preliminary encounters, as it were 'trial runs' with lesser hazards, or smaller
monsters, and has gained confidence from his discovery that he
is always victorious, that power appears to be on his side.

He sets out, sometimes reluctant, sometimes naively enthusiastic, sometimes mocked at or discouraged by others, and
he quickly runs into one kind of danger or another. The dangers
which lie before him tend to be of five, possibly six, kinds;
dangers of seduction, magic, inertia, depression, the brutality of
others, and possibly of starvation. The hero may be persuaded
to forsake his vocation by losing himself in sexual or other
fantasy, by his inability to act, by despair, by his fear of pain,
or by simply lacking the nourishment that is required to keep
body and soul together.

However, he is far from alone in this struggle against desperate
odds, though he often pretends to himself that he is alone. He

has any number of allies who turn up infallibly at twists in the road — old men and old women, girls who are in love with him, talking animals, gods disguised as beggars — and show him how to survive the worst that fate has in store for him.

(Our interest in heroes, it should be remarked at this point, leads us to forget the would-be heroes who don't succeed, who tend to get their heads chopped off, or be consumed by the monster. Where have they gone wrong? The consensus of fairy-tale and fable is that either they should not have set out on the quest in the first place — they were the wrong person or were doing it at the wrong time — or that somehow they spoiled their chance. Apart from the risk of being overcome by the various dangers outlined above, there is the risk of either alienating or ignoring one's allies. If the hero ignores the whining old beggar in the road who asks to share his crust, then he cannot go on to discover that she is a goddess who will give him vital information. Equally, if he is too self-willed to take advice then he may make fatal errors. Sometimes, but by no means always, on the evidence of the stories, he may get a second chance. It seems, therefore, that charity and obedience are essentials of the quest, charity because certain crucial facts are never discovered without it, and obedience because the game has its own rules to which the hero must conform or perish. Without charity and obedience, the hero is like someone on a treasure-hunt who carelessly kicks away vital clues.)

Our admiration for the hero's courage must always be slightly lessened by the way his path is made smooth. The briars part for him, he has a magic sword, or a magic potion, as well as inside information about how to overcome his opponents. And in any case, he is preternaturally strong.

Yet with all his advantages, both natural and magic, he comes sooner or later, to a place where magic is of no use to him, where, without any more defence than the best advice obtainable, he has to make the loneliest and most important part of his journey. It is here that he finds the treasure, or decisively defeats the monster, and here that he runs the greatest danger of never again returning to his old haunts.

The hero has exerted the peculiar fascination he has on the human imagination because each of us recognises an embryo hero within us. Not all of us are interested in literary heroes; we may prefer the 'real life' heroism of the moon explorer or the transatlantic sailor, or be stimulated by the life story of a pop star or footballer. Some, it must be said, are more influenced by the myth than others. Whereas some merely dream of heroic exploits, others try to realise them in their life-style, and actively seek treasure or attack one kind of monster or another. Heroism is careless of personal safety and comfort. A recent report from Russia suggested that, among intellectuals, there is envy among those who have not served a forced spell in a labour camp towards those who have. As so often in the annals of chivalry, dishonour seems much more terrible than the possibility of death.

Some are tempted towards heroism by the need to overcome childhood handicaps — poverty, or physical deformity, or the loss of a parent. For some loneliness is enough. The sense of being 'different', and so cut off from easy and equal intercourse with one's peers, leads into a sense of being 'special', marked out from the others.

In our education of children much emphasis is laid on 'specialness', not only in the way admiration is given to children who excel in one field or another, but in the way in which 'special-ness' in history is singled out and commended. It is, of course, done in a very moral way. We select those who have, on the whole, found paths for their heroism which have benefited the human race — a Florence Nightingale, an Edith Cavell, a Lawrence of Arabia. We do not ask what heroism it took to be a Genghis Khan or a Hitler, in fact we would withhold the word 'hero' from them altogether. The word 'hero' has come to be used almost entirely in an admiring sense; he undertakes his quest 'for the people'. After he undertakes his quest, nothing is ever quite the same again. The 'dark' heroes perhaps have a different, more pathetic function. They are the puppets of the people, manu-factured out of collective anger and guilt.

However, we may have to admit that the heroes of light are not without their puppet aspect. Somebody has to kill the dragon, fight Goliath, awaken the princess, pull the sword out of the stone. Nobody is a more likely volunteer than one who has nur-tured for years a secret dream of 'specialness', and a longing to 'show them' that he is not made of the common clay of all the rest of them.

If the lonely are particularly at risk, it must be said that every man has some experience of being the adventuring hero, and it is this that gives hero myths their universal appeal. Everyone experiences a movement away from infant dependency, and out into a world which is both harsh and rewarding. The growth away from father and mother, the conquering of skills, the endurance of pain, and the enjoyment of pleasure, the attempt at relationship outside the family circle, are in themselves a journey, and give each of us some real knowledge of what journey involves. A novel by Thomas Mann, *The Holy Sinner*, obviously much influenced by Freudian ideas, sees the task of the journeying hero as one of freeing himself from incestuous longing.

It is perhaps only when we look through some such window as Mann's, that the hero can nowadays be wholly acceptable to us. We can admire courage as much as ever, but yet we have an obstinate feeling that the hero is not quite what he seems, and not necessarily what he thinks he is. No sooner nowadays do we call someone a hero than others arise to point out the feet of clay, feet that the heroes themselves would have been at great pains to deny. We are curiously pleased to discover that the heroes are 'no better' than the rest of us, partly because of envy since we have heard the heroes' praises sung repeatedly in our ears like the praise of older and cleverer siblings, but partly because this kind of unbalanced personality has begun to seem to us phony, not human. Perhaps we no longer want people to be marvellous.

It may be too that the events of the past forty years have reminded us how, caught in certain myths, like a fly in a web, heroes are lethal. Nazism, *apartheid*, the I.R.A. brand of nationalism, remind us that one man's myth is another man's murder.

What we have begun to see is that the hero, and the idealisation which surrounds him, stand for something juvenile in us. A Freudian analyst, Roy Schafer, writes of what he called 'the romantic vision' like this: [1]

In the romantic vision . . . life is a quest or a series of quests. The quest is a perilous, heroic individualistic journey. Its destination or goal combines some of all of the qualities of

[1] Roy Schafer, *The Psycho-Analytic Vision of Reality* (*International Journal of Psycho-Analysis*, Vol. 51, 1970, Part III), p. 279.

mystery, grandeur, sacredness, love and possession by or fusion with some higher power or principle (Nature, Virtue, Honour, Beauty, etc.). The seeker is an innocent, adventurous hero, and his quest ends, after crucial struggles, with his exaltation. . . . The standard cowboy movie is a commonplace, communal American expression of romantic vision.

The quest follows the pattern of the wish-fulfilling day-dream (and the analyst would add masturbation fantasy). In this daydream ideals are represented by virtuous heroes and heroines while threats to the ascendancy of these ideals are embodied in villains. The romantic vision is, implicitly if not explicitly, regressive and childlike, particularly in its persistent nostalgia for a golden age in time or space that is the essential destination of the quest, the prize for the counterphobic victor in the central conflict. Outwardly, it may proclaim as its achievement a discontinuous leap forward in existence and thereby an emancipation from history; superficially this proclamation obscures its regressiveness and its quality . . . of being ultimately atemporal or ahistorical.

Other common manifestations of the romantic vision are the idealization of individuality and 'nature': self-expression is uncritically and totalistically equated with triumph, and narcissistic or impulsive action with being 'natural' (or 'authentic' or 'with it'). In fact, idealization of any sorts is a romantic phenomenon.

The hero is a simple soul, living in a simple world in which friends and enemies, goodness and badness, are clearly defined. All his encounters are personally viewed, and in a sense the world exists for his convenience, to make a backdrop for his adventures. It is the stage for his 'specialness', and perhaps more painful than death for him would be the discovery that he is not 'special' at all, but is only one among many heroes all equally hell- or heaven-bent on achieving their object in the face of all odds.

At this point we must look again at the fact that so few women, at least in literature, have been accorded heroic status. Women are either the unlucky victims of predators, as with little Red Riding-Hood, or the many girls threatened by dragons and monsters, or they are the prize the hero wins after breaking through the briars, or surviving the tests devised by the princess's father (a kind of tangible First Class Honours). Or they are witches like Medea or Circe, who can be powerful allies or deathly enemies. They are either helpless nonentities or they are very powerful, holding information that is vital to the hero.

If quests are a masturbatory fantasy, as Schafer suggests, and the male fantasy is one of conquering the world and making it subject to his own 'specialness', then it would look as if the female fantasy might be one either of being conquered or of achieving a subtler and more sophisticated kind of power than the male hero. This is her 'specialness'. If at first sight we get the impression that the woman is more 'grown up' than the man because she does not indulge in a narcissistic vision of the world as her stage, then we must think again. She is as much caught up in the romantic dream as her male partner.

The stage on which these two now act out their drama is in many ways so utterly different from the world of medieval questing. The most striking and all-pervading difference of all lies in the contemporary spirit of disillusion. Of course, it is not the first time in history that men have been disillusioned, and we know that periods of hope alternate with periods of despair, periods of faith with periods of scepticism. But any period of disillusion is *ipso facto* hostile to the romantic spirit, an irruption of reality through the crust of idealisation. There are many who do not like reality (none of us find it continuously bearable, as Eliot has pointed out), and who try to tempt us back into earlier forms of romanticism and idealisation sensing, no doubt, that this avoids facing the really hard questions about morals, faith, and personal wholeness. They want light (or Light) but not darkness, and must therefore distract us as best they can from the terrible task of trying to assimilate our own darkness. But the spirit of the times is, fortunately, against them. Artists, writers, composers, as well as many ordinary people in their everyday lives prefer their disillusion to artificial illumination and welcome the many forms of experiment in personal relations, knowing that this route, painful and disillusioning as it often is in itself, is no longer one we can ignore.

Though we embrace our disillusion, it is nevertheless a terrible state to be in, a state of hopeless expectancy, an apparent impotence which it is difficult to believe can ever yield to creativity. What we know, we know at a ruinous price.

> What is the price of experience? [asks Blake.] It is bought
>   with the price
> Of all that a man hath, his house, his wife, his children.
> Wisdom is sold in the desolate market where none come to
>   buy,
> And in the wither'd field where the farmer plows for bread
>   in vain.[2]

We know that wither'd field with a joyless intimacy; so many of the harvests have failed though the seeds were planted with love and hope. Our dreams of empire, our liberal beliefs, our hopes of brotherhood, our intentions of sharing, our vision of racial brotherhood, our wishes for progress, our plans for dominating and controlling nature have each been blighted to the point where we know that none of them alone can feed and comfort us. Only the wilfully blind still claim that one of these quests can save us, insisting the more fanatically as others ask the difficult questions. There are many who are wilfully blind, many right-wing or left-wing heroes, many who pin their faith to politics, or religion, or humanism, or science. The agony of living without hope is too great for them.

The problem is that neither they nor we will admit that we are in a quite new situation. Orwell castigated, rightly in my opinion, those who insisted that there is nothing new under the sun, that whatever happens to us it has all happened before. (He thought the stronghold of this outlook was Catholicism, but it does show its head elsewhere.) When voices have been raised to suggest that what is happening to us has not happened before, others with the kind of cynicism which Orwell hated, have sneered at the melodramaticism of this, the unhistoricity of it. Mention a mass-killing or a private aberration, an unusual personality or a bizarre set of circumstances, and they will give you chapter and verse to show that it has all happened before. For them time is cyclic and man never changes, and this takes away some of the pain and some of the responsibility. If man is that kind of creature then nothing anyone can do will make much difference. Modern

---

[2] William Blake, 'The Four Zoas' (Second Night).

developments make our destructiveness more efficient, that is all. The invention of trains, and the discovery of nuclear fission, made Auschwitz and Hiroshima possible as they would not have been otherwise, but was the fate of those who died there any more terrible they would argue, or really any different from that of the countless numbers of men, women and children who have died over the centuries when a hostile tribe or army swept through their village, killing, raping, and burning?

But just because cruelty and suffering are similar wherever they occur we need not ignore some of the more terrible intuitions which come to us in the present situation. The most terrible of all is that we are not just repeating an uncomfortable pattern but are approaching a crisis of ultimate magnitude which it is highly problematic whether the human race, or anyhow civilisation, will survive. (One commentator has suggested that in the event of a nuclear war the only people likely to survive are the tribes of Central Africa where the rainfall is almost non-existent. The people of these tribes are still at the Stone Age level of development and left to themselves on this planet would presumably, over millions of years, evolve a civilisation.) It would be foolish if we denied this possibility, out of fear of megalomania, of thinking ourselves and our situation more 'special' than it is.

What is it that is special about our situation? Our greatest danger may lie in the fact that the answers are so obvious that we will ignore them rather as children sometimes ignore gross physical handicaps and mobilise their other capacities to try to overcome the fault. Yet we need to notice, painfully and in detail, what we have lost if we are to know about any kind of wholeness of living.

For example, the population explosion is killing, slowly and systematically, our ability to empathise in the suffering of others. Germaine Greer has described a bishop, comfortably eating a large meal at a public luncheon, speaking about the floods in East Bengal as 'the first of the irreversible disasters'. He did no more than any of us, forced for our own sanity's sake to shut out the screams, the swollen bellies, the woebegone faces from our consciousness because there are too many of them. We have not yet devised a formula to deny their suffering, as did the Victorians with such sentiments as 'The rich man in his castle, the poor man at his gate' but we may well produce our own version in time.

Hunger, the primary fear in each of us, must continue to spread as populations grow. There is nothing new or original about this fact; it feels almost trite to offer it. But we are never without its shadow. Everything that is said and done stands judged in the appalling knowledge of the population explosion.

There are the other, equally trite, problems which stem from the fact that there are just too many of us. A country like Great Britain which is small, heavily populated, and which has enjoyed a stable and settled way of life for centuries, is well placed to know the pain of this before larger countries begin to feel the pinch. Since the war, despite all that has been achieved in such schemes as slum clearance, we have watched the steady destruction of British social culture, and an appalling deterioration in our way of life. The comments of 'Release' about urban environment apply equally to suburban environment. Older cities, except for a very few with strong and visionary City Councils, have yielded to the pressures of industry and the crying need for housing, and allowed much that gave character and distinctiveness and human warmth to their streets to disappear. The enormous increase in road traffic has meant a vastly more complex road system, much of it destructive of countryside and buildings that were precious to those who lived amongst them. The crying need for what politicians sentimentally call 'homes' has meant the construction of huge estates, often to the cheapest possible specification, which have made tragic inroads on our diminishing countryside. The most depressing aspect of it all is that there is no foreseeable end to it. In order to fill the leaking bucket many more large cities will have to be built before the end of the century, and what this involves, quite simply, is the total destruction of the countryside.

Meanwhile the growing population needs more jobs, more schools, more food, more possessions, and more public utilities. The difficulty of disposing of the refuse of humanity becomes ever more acute; sewage, industrial waste, and the rubbish which attends every family and its daily life become major problems. Paper, particularly paper used for the packaging of foodstuffs, tin-cans, and bottles all become an intolerable nuisance.

Overcrowding persecutes and plagues the town-dweller, subjecting him to humiliations like strap-hanging in the Tube, making him compete fiercely and at a high price for living space, forcing him to queue to eat, or to get out of the supermarket. Desmond Morris has pointed out how rats kept in overcrowded conditions become viciously aggressive towards one another, and he has applied this to the situation of urban man. There are always dangers in suggesting that rats and men are analogous, but few who have lived in modern big cities will deny the deterioration of manners and fellowship.

Along with the deterioration of fellowship goes, naturally enough, loneliness, and alongside loneliness is the proliferation of mental illnesses which seem to germinate in these conditions.

Then there is the range of stress conditions which seem to emerge in overcrowded conditions, indicating perhaps that man responds to over-population by extreme competitiveness. Competitiveness in work, in education, in the number and quality of our possessions, suggests that we do not resign ourselves to getting lost in the crowd; we are going to be noticed if it is the last thing we do. Which it very well may be, since stress is apt to shorten our lives either by diseases directly affected by it like heart disease, or by diseases which come from addictions like cigarettes or alcohol.

Family life, marriage, and that most sensitive indicator of our happiness and sense of well-being, sexual contentment, all become victims of our torment.

The sense that life is changing rapidly about us makes it more difficult to hold on to stability in relationships. When everything about is in a state of change, often, though not invariably, for the worse, it is difficult to preserve the hopefulness and patience which love demands, difficult not to try to grab what one wants, or thinks one wants, while there is still time, or before someone else grabs it.

If life is, in general, unsatisfying then we begin to demand more, perhaps intolerably much, of our sexual and marital relationships. A man or woman who does a satisfying job, who has a sense of belonging to a close community in which he or she is known and valued, and who finds living conditions congenial and conducive to contentment, can afford far more tolerance of a partner, or of children, than someone in a state of general frustration. Contentment leads to an inner peace in which relationship can take root.

A high degree of discontent leads inevitably to violence, which is an attempt to impose one's own will out of the need (the necessity it feels) to get the emotional, material or political response of one's choice. While society must protect itself against the raging and often aberrant self-will of individual members, it is idle to talk, as hard-liners do, as if all that is needed is an iron hand. In the present situation, in which many have genuine cause for discontent, violence is inevitable, and savage and repressive measures can only make it worse. It is like trying to deal with the steam in a kettle by blocking all the holes.

It seems to me similarly foolish to suggest that the obscene films, photographs, books, and sexual displays, which worry certain groups of the community so deeply, need only to be banned to resolve our sexual problems. The extraordinary commercial success of all these undertakings can, of course, be represented as evidence of man's wickedness, a wickedness which we should be irresponsible to encourage. But what their success also undoubtedly reveals is how obsessed we are with sexual fantasies, more particularly with sado-masochistic fantasies. We should scarcely lap up the amount of cruelty we do, much of it from 'respectable' sources such as television, the major cinema circuits, and well-known publishers, if the theme was entirely boring and repugnant to us. At the time of writing the B.B.C. have just completed the serialisation of the Victorian school story, *Tom Brown's Schooldays*, touching up some of the sadistic scenes in the original, and introducing many more violent scenes of their own invention. In answer to complaints the director answered that only thus could the story be made viewable to a modern audience, but in any case the audience rating was exceptionally high.

There are very great difficulties in admitting and allowing for our own, or other people's taste for cruelty, the most serious of them being that refined techniques can be seen and copied in real life. The Moors Murder evidence showed that Brady and his accomplice had learned from the books they had read and utilised their knowledge in the torturing of the child. There is also evidence, though of a very small quantity, of children employing techniques seen on television to bully companions, as well

as occasionally employing such techniques on themselves in
suicide attempts.

It would seem as if we have arrived at a crossroads in our
treatment of the theme of cruelty on contemporary entertainment. We can either stir up public indignation against it, and
insist upon a much more rigorous censorship, or we can continue much as we are doing, with what is really a *laisser-faire*
policy, perhaps in the discovery that sado-masochistic fantasies
are a very common phenomenon and do not as a rule issue in the
torturing of others or ourselves, or at least not by the direct
routes outlined in the fantasies.

If we follow the first course, possibly applying censorship only
to the more blatant types of torture and cruelty, do we really
stand any chance of success? The very great popularity of material
dealing with cruelty means that those whom we would need to
marshal to oppose it would often be the same people who secretly
enjoy it, a hypocritical situation by no means uncommon in this
field. The most amusing example of this approach to violence,
cruelty and sexual aberration is the *News of the World* which
feels a need morally to justify the hair-raising tales that it tells
by shaking its head and tutting over the very material which is
its main preoccupation. But even if we could apply the most
rigorous standards of censorship, would it work? I think this unlikely, since the commercial success of such fantasies, and the
public obsessions which underlie it, are now too well known.
What we pushed out by the front door would creep in at the
back. What was denied in respectable theatres and cinemas and
bookshops would reappear in a thousand sleazier places, with
the inevitability of bootleg liquor during Prohibition. What was
forbidden in the form of novels or television plays would reappear
as descriptions of 'real life' events or as 'news'. Unhappily there
has been and continues to be enough torture in the twentieth-
century world to feed any number of fantasies. While the public
demand remains high it would be impossible to ban violence in
entertainment; the same fantasies would merely leak into other
channels of communication where they would be harder to detect.

This does not mean, in my view, that we are condemned to a
monotonous diet of cruelty for the rest of our natural lives.
Public champions of morality always seem to ignore the part that
fashion plays in our lives, the way that veins of interest and taste

inexorably become worked out, so that after a while no one can clearly recall even what the fascination was all about.

This is presumably because certain aspects of our collective personality have been trying to emerge into consciousness. They cannot do this without exaggeration and over-statement, but once the statement has been made and noted, once that is, that particular facts have been taken note of by the conscious mind, then it is time to move on. This leads us to the possibility that we are collectively trying to perceive something about cruelty as it relates to ourselves, that, like all masturbatory fantasies, cruelty contains seeds of revelation for us. Coaxed to grow instead of being stamped upon they might reveal something about the nature of our poverty which would lead to its correction.

Sado-masochism apart, there has been a vast increase of interest in sexuality in all its many forms, and 'sex-shops', informative books and films, and books which encouraged a more adventurous approach to intercourse have abounded. Again, the sheer force of fashion seem to be a phenomenon to be treated with respect. Those who represent the public as pitiful simpletons, gulled by wicked commercial interests who make money out of titillation, seem to ignore the difficulty of selling a customer anything that he does not already want. The commercial interests *do* make money out of titillation, of course, but it is hard to see how they could do so, at least on the scale they do, if their matter was deeply repugnant to the public. The only customers from whom they would be unlikely to make money would be those already so satisfied with the sexual encounters that life afforded them that they could not be bothered to seek substitutes in films or books. The high sales of pornographic literature is eloquent, and pitiful, testimony of the true state of affairs.

What it indicates is that, far from being bold and permissive the majority of us are 'hung-up' in our sexual lives, troubled by the spectres of impotence and frigidity, lacerated by guilt, plagued by ignorance. When marriage was a stronger institution, it was easier for men and women to conceal their dissatisfaction, either because some pleasure was achieved by the sense of doing the correct thing by society, so that it seemed best to convey to others the impression that all was well, or because illicit sexual encounters supplied what one's official relationship lacked. There is now a greater impatience with these forms of hypocrisy, a

greater awareness of what is irreparably lost if one is sexually
starved, and a refusal to endure such suffering if there is any other
solution. No amount of insistence on 'Christian standards' is
going to get this particular cat back inside the bag, the bag of
pretending either that people did not need sex or that nearly all
marriages were sexually satisfying.

It is not only sexually that our relationships have failed, of
course, though sex, as always, is a wonderfully reliable guide to
what a person is about in the general conduct of his life. In our
loss of formality in nearly all forms of relationship we have un-
covered the poverty of loving and sharing which is the reality of our
lives — poverty between husband and wife, parents and children,
between friends and colleagues and neighbours. It is often only
when desperation has broken up a situation — in the form of
illness, divorce, suicide, addiction, crime, running away from
home, the use of physical force, professional failure — that any
real intimacy seems to be achieved, and by then it may be too
late to be fully effective.

I am not at all sure that this poverty is a new thing. It may be
that our ancestors were better at concealing it than we are,
strongly supported by more rigid social and religious pressures.
If so, then we may be luckier than they were. Since we are
forced to admit our poverty, our own failure at loving, then we
can perhaps take measures to correct it.

If we don't have to pretend that our marriages are a supreme
success, or that our relations with our children are as good as
they might be, then at once we are freer, released by admitting
our own self-contempt as well as our rage against our partners or
relatives. 'Love' becomes an altogether more vivid possibility.

What tends to be so stifling in marriage is resentment, bottled
up for years, emitted like a bad smell in irritability and small
remarks designed to wound and undermine. Wherever real growth
and hope is perceived in the other the delicate plant must be
trampled upon since it arouses intolerable envy and fear of
exclusion.

It is such poverty as this (very often expressing itself through
extra-marital relationships) that many of the most perceptive
films and plays about marriage have addressed themselves to
in recent years, reaping torrents of abuse from those who prefer a more simplistic view of human relations.

We cannot easily tolerate the idea of freedom, freedom for our husband or wife, freedom for our children, freedom for our fellow citizens, or freedom for ourselves. Specially not freedom for ourselves. Like the Bermudan slaves of the nineteenth century we will not take freedom, even when it is a gift, but continue working under the old system, as if nothing had happened.

Yet there are signs of change — signs of attempt at new life styles, and signs that women, in particular, feel that their role as hitherto understood is too limited. It is no longer possible to present childbearing as an unmitigated blessing conferred by women upon a grateful society, and even the task of caring for children in their early years which we have come to believe is of more crucial importance in the children's development than our ancestors would have thought, is seen to be over fairly early in a woman's working life. So that inevitably women are thinking again about their contribution to society, and in many cases are finding the traditional fulfilment of housekeeper and helpmate as well as mother insufficient. Some real sharing of the domestic tasks with men is being insisted upon by Women's Lib., so that women may, if they wish, be freer to undertake professional or other work outside the home.

In looking at the world as it is still left for heroes to explore or conquer, I have not mentioned what to many would seem the most significant thing about our present discontent — our lack of a religious faith.

This is not in itself anything new. Ever since the Renaissance men have struggled publicly with their doubts about God. Montaigne nobly rested his case upon doubt, since this is all that he could honestly attest to. Descartes, having arranged his own catharsis of doubt, nevertheless managed to save God from the wreck of so much else.

Mankind has passed through many periods of scepticism since Descartes tried to put in a good word for God, periods in which we have tried every brand of Christianity and every brand of agnosticism and atheism. When I speak of the uniqueness of our time, one of the things which I regard as evidence of this is that we seem, for the first time, to be on the far side of the traditional controversies about the existence or otherwise of God. 'Religious' people (to use an old-fashioned expression which is fast changing its meaning) are, in general, far less insistent than they used to be that others must see what they see and do what they do. Agnostics and atheists are correspondingly less dogmatic. Perhaps what each has begun to know (though neither yet has begun to articulate it) is the extraordinary ambiguity of the religious experience (and often, one must add, of life itself). In this area it is possible for men to say opposite things and still describe the same truth; it is possible for them to say the same things and mean something entirely different. What matters is their individual method of seeking.

One of the astonishing discoveries for those brought up in dogmatic frameworks is that those brought up in other dogmatic frameworks which purport to offer a totally different view of the world tend, by hard experiencing, to arrive at the same spiritual intuitions as they have themselves. Assured that theirs is the only safe route they find that others have made the journey while neglecting every one of their own precautions, but observing rules which never occurred to them. It would seem as if there are many starting off points for journey; it can be one of the great religions, or one of the smaller and crankier ones; it can be science; it can be art; it can be psychoanalysis; it can be personal joy or tragedy of especial magnitude. Sooner or later the routes converge, and perhaps sooner or later they run necessarily through one another's territory as if each is needed to complete the journey.

What makes it so difficult to talk rationally about afterwards is the fact that whatever route we begin by becomes for us a holy and unique route. Remembering what we remember, it is only with the utmost difficulty that we can learn that to others their route seems equally holy and essential. In fact, to begin with we cannot see that this is so, and are only likely to do so if fate, or inclination, throws us into the company of those who do not share our framework. It is always bewildering, sometimes threatening, to discover that others think and feel in a very different way from ourselves, but it is necessary to explore this difference deeply and respectfully to get to the point of knowing that we are also very alike. In the early stages we have to learn a kind of translation, transposing what others have learned in a different framework into what we know from our own experience. After a while we can learn to think in other languages besides our native one, and note that different languages often illuminate one another. There is no need to fall into the sentimental error of supposing we can borrow a few words of one and use it like slang, or pidgin English, to make ourselves more vividly understood. The languages are all distinctive, with grammars and idioms of their own which must be painstakingly learned.

The religious dogmatists will, I think, be the ones who find the validity of other languages most painful. They have for so long been sure that theirs was the primary, if not the only language, that the humility involved in sharing meaning with others who have taken a wholly different route, is almost unbearable. Pick up almost any book by a Christian theologian, priest or layman which examines the contemporary situation in terms of what religion has to offer, and it will bear the marks of belief that others cannot get along without their help and contribution. This is as striking where the writers are deeply concerned with the problems of modern life as where they only reveal interest in a closed system of theology.

A book, for example, like Kenneth Leech's *Pastoral Care and the Drug Scene* which shows a meticulous knowledge of the drug problem in our society, and a wonderfully sympathetic care of those suffering from addiction, manages to suggest that social problems can only be cured if translated into a Christian language and given a Christian remedy.

The Church in its pastoral care is not simply concerned with the counselling and guidance of individuals, but primarily with the building up of the body of Christ. Too much emphasis has been placed, within the current 'pastoral care' movements, on a clinical model, which sees 'sickness' as a private disturbance, and shows little understanding of the social forces and the community structure. This has been particularly so in the case of drug addicts, where many Christians have tended to see the 'drug subculture' as wholly evil, and have regarded the extrication of the addict from his environment as the fundamental prerequisite of 'rehabilitation'.... The theological principle behind the Church's involvement in the inner city crisis districts is that the drug-taking subcultures can only be truly redeemed from within. The Church's role therefore is not to rescue and isolate individual members (though it should be emphasized that this is often a necessary stage in healing), but to build within the subcultural groups the structures of spiritual renewal. This is the pattern of the Incarnation, the self-annihilation of God within the suffering of humanity: only when the grain of wheat dies into the earth does resurrection become possible. The central task then is the creation of a community in which if one member suffers all suffer, a community characterized by the sharing of bread and of all life, and this creation is the work of the Spirit, using the members of the body.

It is unfair to choose this passage since it is typical of hundreds of others by less sensitive writers illustrating what I believe is a pretentious strain in Christian thought difficult to perceive since it is linked to a wish to serve others. There is an unconscious superiority in the assumption that one (or one's Church) has a unique contribution to give to others, and that they must take it in the form in which it is presented or it will be the worse for them. There is no hint that the same task — the creation of a community whose members find life good enough not to be tempted to suicide by addiction — might be attempted or achieved by quite other means, political, educational, sociological, or psycho-analytical. Suppose it *was* attempted by some such other method with no mention of Christianity, and the method was found to be a success, would the result still be the same? Would it be true that something analogous to the Incarnation had happened? In my view, yes, though perhaps not in Fr. Leech's.

In the end, one's point of view depends upon whether or not one believes there are two races of men, the Christians and the others, or only one race of men, the human. If one takes the latter view then it is not necessary to put everything into Christian jargon. Crucifixion and resurrection is the common lot of man, whether or not he knows the words. If Christianity is our native tongue then that may be the way we want to talk about what we see around us, but if we have begun from a different vantage-point then our language will be different.

What we all have in common is experience, of joy and pain, hope and disappointment, shame and gladness.

There used to be a joke told at the expense of the Roman Catholics in which St. Peter was showing a new arrival around heaven. He introduced him to one sect after another, and then

they arrived at a large enclosure with a high wall around it.
'Keep your voice down', said St. Peter. 'They like to think
they're the only ones here.'
For Roman Catholics read Christians.

Perhaps the most irritating thing about the Christians is their
insistence on their helpfulness. Putting oneself in the position of
helper is an extraordinarily skilful way of always being superior
to others, always knowing better and being in a position of
strength while others are in a position of weakness. There is no
hint, for example, in the above passage, or indeed in the whole
book, that a Christian might be a drug addict or vulnerable to
some other form of suicide; he is too busy having all the answers
and showing others how to do it. To that extent he has abne-
gated his humanity, the humanity that is inseparable from being
at one's wits end, from enduring one's ignorance, from making a
fool of oneself, from accepting that others may know better or at
least as well. In a skilful attack on Christian invulnerability, the
poet Stevie Smith projects this superiority on to the person of
Christ:

> Was he married, did he try
> To support as he grew less fond of them
> Wife and family?
>
> No,
> He never suffered such a blow.
>
> Did he feel pointless, feeble and distrait,
> Unwanted by everyone and in the way?
>
> From his cradle he was purposeful,
> His bent strong and his mind full.
>
> . . . Did he feel strong
> Pain for being wrong?
>
> He was not wrong, he was right, . . .
> He suffered from others', not his own, spite.

But there *is* no suffering like having made a mistake
Because of being of an inferior make.

He was not inferior,
He was superior . . .

Rejecting this unpleasant idol, Stevie Smith turns gratefully back
to ordinary humanity and the courage it shows without hope of
supernatural support or interference.

All human beings should have a medal,
A god cannot carry it, he is not able.[3]

The sad thing is that, despite the justified indignation of this
poem, the Christians do have a very good language for talking
about being human, a language of beauty and subtlety that is
sensitive to all sorts of nuances and moods. It is only when they
talk in the accents of propaganda that the language sounds false.
Many clergy still talk, particularly when discussing a medium like
television, as if faith is a commodity to be sold like soap powder
with winning advertisements. The language of campaigns, and
strategy to 'win people over' is also common in Christian circles,
the human soul being seen as a bastion to be captured by force,
or a prize on a bingo stall.

All talk of 'winning' people, of making a good case for
Christianity, seems to me to be deeply irreligious, failing in the
utter respect needed towards the inviolateness of human beings,
and often failing in truth. Failing too in any real grasp of the
importance of 'ripeness' in all human decisions and events. People
will take what they need from us or from others at the time they
are ripe to do so; love means an absolute refusal to apply pressure
to others, however much we may imagine it is for their own
good.

To talk of 'redeeming the drug-taking subculture', of 'building
structures of spiritual renewal' and similar phrases which are
widely used in religious/sociological literature also seems painfully inflated, beginning from the quite unwarranted assumption
(so far as we can so far see) that Christians have worked out any
answers to the peculiar problems which confront us, or have any

[3] Stevie Smith, *Selected Poems* (Longmans, 1962).

better idea of how and where to start building than anyone else. Become closely acquainted with any church group, or any group of clergy, and you will find no fewer personality problems than you find anywhere else. Sometimes faith can be a help in facing problems, sometimes it can prevent people facing them; it does not eliminate them, and this is a mercy, since it sets limits to human arrogance.

A few churchmen, such as Alistair Kee, have begun to face the fact that no amount of strategy is going to 'win' people, and in *The Way of Transcendence* he has tried to work out a path for those who cannot see eye to eye with him theologically, what he calls 'Christian Faith without Belief in God'. Like Leech, he has a secret agenda. What he would *really* like is for everyone to have a faith just like his own, and he has moments of thinking they would be in this happy condition if they had a proper chance. 'The challenge of Jesus Christ, if put directly to people today, would be a meaningful challenge.'[4] On the other hand, it seems it is not to be. 'The vast majority of people in this country today have never had the chance to choose for or against Christ'[5] so *faute de mieux* they have to be offered something less than the full diet.

It is interesting that the diet Kee selects is that of Christian faith without God. Following a number of contemporary theologians he feels that God is a well-nigh impossible concept for modern man. Altizer felt that God died at the Incarnation, Hamilton that God is absent, Tillich that God does not exist in the facile way that we have supposed, and many lesser men without the advantages of these find the whole idea of God meaningless. Yet Kee does not like to see modern man without a faith, and gives a good reason why not. 'There is a widespread search for an object worthy of faith, and a healthy mistrust of that blind faith in leaders and causes which has proved so disastrous in this century. The attraction of such faith is not that it brings personal responsibility to an end, but rather that a goal worthy of total commitment brings new dimensions to life.'[6] So that his answer is to admit that God has been thrown overboard, and to sub-

---

[4] Alistair Kee, *The Way of Transcendence: Christian Faith without Belief in God* (Penguin, 1971).
[5] Ibid.
[6] Ibid.

stitute a Christian faith based, presumably, on respect for Jesus. This answer is a strange, and perhaps revealing one. If he had gone, not to theologians and academics but to the Underground he would have found that the opposite answer would be more likely to be of help. God is not a difficult idea there, and neither is Jesus, (though it is doubtful whether Jesus is seen in terms of 'challenges' and 'decisions', words which have a muscular ring reminiscent of *Scouting for Boys*). What would be unacceptable is precisely the nostrum that Kee recommends — the Christian faith, in so far as this is seen as an exclusive and prescriptive system (like, for instance, being a Conservative), rather than a possible method of making sense of what was happening to one. Is it unkind to suggest that, in the present state of religious ship-wreck, this theologian prefers to throw God overboard rather than see the ship go down with both God and Christianity on board?

Others, however, prefer God, or anyhow 'a sense of religion'. John-Michael Tebelak, the man responsible for *Godspell*, the rock musical which derives its inspiration from Christian myth, talked about it like this: 'I never feel the show is purely Christian; I just like to think of it as universal. It is not important to be a Christian in order to enjoy it, that is part of the point. . . . *Godspell* does not try to convert anyone. The Church has failed to do that. We are not trying to change anybody's views; we are just trying to give them a sense of religion.' Tebelak found himself 'turned on' by reading the gospels, he says. 'I felt some kind of commitment.'

'A sense of religion' is the interesting phrase. What Tebelak and others regard as the growing point is the sense of the numinous, a sense which may, or may not include certainties about God, or dogmatic beliefs about Christ, still less any commitment to organised religion. It is this which shows a man his 'myth', the particular journey which is for him, and which others can only guess at. Like Abraham or Moses he is led out into the unknown. Like Moses in particular he will err and lose his way through fear and through awe; the pressure of the numinous is not easy to bear.

This is, of course, very close to Jung's theory of individuation, and equally close to the wealth of folk-legend and myth with which man has surrounded himself. It is a 'sense of religion'

which has led men out, in the cause of true love no less than in
overtly religious causes, and in the moments of ecstasy (unity)
which these journeys have afforded, they have known that the
god is present.

It may matter much less than we have thought that men make
the journeys along prescribed paths, or feel able to make conventional declarations about God; these possibilities, in any case,
are often prescribed or counter-prescribed by temperament and
early upbringing. The prescribed paths are essential to some, but
fatal to others, who must find their own communities, gospels,
sermons and gurus.

But what about Schafer's criticism of the heroic journey and
its idealisation as a romantic dream, based upon an exaggerated
individualism? There is much in Jung's description of individuation, and certainly much in Jung's own view of his life, as
revealed in his autobiographical book *Memories, Dreams and
Reflections* which fits Schafer's criticism. Romanticism is unlikely to serve us at all adequately in our present predicament, and
if Schafer's diagnosis is correct we should do well to sift all the
prescriptions offered to us, whether in the form of 'individuation'
theories, formal religion, informal religion, or the new life-styles
of the Underground.

First, however, let us see what Schafer considers to be the
alternative to the romantic journey or quest. As an analyst he
makes the interesting point that when patients come to him for
analysis it is very often because they have become aware that
their personal quest has failed. Whatever previously gave meaning
to their lives no longer works for them, and the goals which
once seemed attainable 'remain ambiguous, elusive and costly'.
A sense of inauthenticity pervades them, and in this post-
romantic mood they are ready to look for help in a way that they
were not before. Is the journey then over? No, but it becomes
very different.

The quest continues, but, for the patient, the dragons change,
the modes of combat change, and the concepts of heroism and
victory change. More and more the dangers and adversaries
are seen to be repressed infantile experiences and fantasies,
unconscious identifications and introjects, and infantile
defences and motives for defence. . . . As the analysis deepens,

the ordeal to be lived through and the victory to be won concern not so much a hostile and rigid environment, and not so much reaching the analytic 'moment of truth', but immersion into a disturbing inner world that is a highly distorted version of an earlier environment and earlier selves. Gaining insight into this world replaces much interpersonal and intrapersonal aggressive and libidinal manipulation as the way to fight it all out. Heroic fulfilling of tasks becomes 'working through' in the face of sometimes almost intolerable anxiety, guilt, grief, yearning and despair. And the actual reward? A more united subjective self, one which has more room in it for undisguised pleasure, to be sure, but also for control, delay, decisive renunciations, remorse, mourning, memories, anticipations, ideas and moral standards; and more room too, for a keen sense of real challenges, dangers and rewards in one's current existence. The childlike, regressive nostalgia is reduced in influence as is the attachment to dragons — for what is a nostalgic counterphobic hero without his dragon?[7]

The romantic vision is not entirely lost — the sense of optimistic quest is carried forward, and with it something courageous and revisionist. What is gone is the old simplisticism and *naïveté*; life is now known to be complex, ambiguous and paradoxical.

It is in this knowledge that, according to Schafer, a man moves on into a deeper vision of what he is about, a vision imbued with tragic and ironic knowledge.

The tragic vision is expressed in a keen responsiveness to the great dilemmas, paradoxes, ambiguities, and uncertainties pervading human action and subjective experience. It manifests itself in alertness to the inescapable dangers, terrors, mysteries and absurdities of existence. It requires one to recognise the elements of defeat in victory and of victory in defeat; the pain in pleasure and the pleasure in pain; the guilt in apparently justified action; the loss of opportunities entailed by every choice and by growth in any direction; the inevitable clashes between passion and duty; the reversal of fortune that hovers over those who are proud or happy or

[7] *The Psycho-Analytic Vision of Reality.*

worthy owing to its being in the nature of people to be inclined to reverse their own fortunes as well as to be vulnerable to accident and unforeseen consequences of their acts and the acts of others.

Schafer believes the tragic vision to be the most searching perspective on human affairs, and he suggests that traditional Christianity has denied it, and found refuge in the romantic vision 'inasmuch as it promises a happy ending, a negation of worldly existence, a clear ultimate meaning or a grand design'. Christianity also has links with a comic vision, the vision according to which 'no dilemma is too great to be resolved, no obstacle too firm to stand against effort and good intentions, no evil so unmitigated and entrenched that it is irremediable, no suffering so intense that it cannot be relieved, and no loss so final that it cannot be undone or made up for'. The tragic vision, by contrast, does believe that losses can be final and irremediable.

Alongside the tragic vision is the ironic vision. It overlaps the tragic vision in its concern with contradiction, ambiguity and paradox, but whereas the tragic vision is taken up with the noble and the demonic, with pity and terror, the ironic vision aims at detachment. It will take neither itself nor others too seriously, and it uncovers the pretention in the romantic and comic visions. 'The very terms of tragic thinking — heroic, demonic, achievement, waste, etc. — are challenged by irony as to their largeness, urgency, clarity, meaningfulness.' Irony saves us as individuals, as well as collectively from 'folie de grandeur'. We are to think ourselves and the events which concern us as supremely important, and the ironic vision reminds us that we matter less than we think.

What do these contrasting visions show us but that if we are still to have a journey then it must change its nature or be totally inadequate to the world in which we find ourselves. We have tried the comic vision and the romantic vision and found that these by themselves no longer seem authentic in our situation. The comic vision covers political solutions, and solutions which depend upon scientific or technological progress, or any view of man which sees him as inevitably progressing. The comic vision selects the more optimistic aspects of a situation, the 'short-cuts', and ignores more complex factors. It would include such diverse methods as behavioural psychology, medicine depending heavily upon drugs and surgery, and religion which places most of its emphasis upon conversion. Some of these solutions and methods still have a place in our struggles for life, some a very important place, but in general they are too simplistic to stand alone, and need to be deepened with a more reflective approach and a less naive understanding.

The romantic vision achieved its finest flowering in the Middle Ages and is movingly illustrated in the myths of unsatisfied love and of pious quests which I already quoted. It has lingered on in a number of movements, more particularly those which depend on a nostalgic appeal. Catholicism, and even more Anglo-Catholicism, has been strongly imbued with it, but any movement which derives its appeal from trying to persuade men to live as their ancestors did, or as people lived in some lost golden age, is marked with romanticism. Romanticism also tends to be individualistic, to play upon man's enjoyment of seeing himself as a lonely figure, battling against unfair odds. Psychoanalysis itself has sometimes been attacked on these grounds — it undoubtedly has its romantic streak. A development from the psychoanalytic approach has been a school of thought about madness, as set out in the writings of R. D. Laing, in which the psychotic person is seen as the lone champion of sane values in a mad world — the schizophrenic as hero.

Much of our present bewilderment could be said to derive from our awareness that these solutions will not do. They have their place, and have served, or still continue to serve their turn, but do not reach our present need. We could be said to have reached the stage at which Schafer says that patients often come into analysis, the moment when the sense of failed quest, of inauthenticity, has become unbearable. If we pursue the analogy then what we need collectively is to be immersed in the disturbing inner world that we would give anything to avoid, in order to gain the insights that would set us free from simplistic notions of ourselves and others.

What seems to lend at least a shred of likelihood to my guess that this is where we are at, is the way that we seem to be flooded with material from our disturbing inner worlds — in the form of violence, pornography, obscenity, etc. Resistance to it, in the form of public anger, is intensifying as it does when we do not want to recognise our own repressions.

But if we are to 'get on', as it were, to the tragic and ironic visions, then there may be no other route. I suppose there may be those who would rather preserve the comic and romantic visions, but it would look as if nothing less than the tragic vision will meet what confronts us — the irreversible tragedies of which the bishop spoke. Neither the comic nor the romantic vision will sustain us as we consider Auschwitz or Hiroshima, Aberfan or East Bengal; indeed it may be that both these visions have played their part in bringing them about. We need a vision which need neither ignore agony, nor take refuge in the dream that in a better organised world it wouldn't happen. We need a vision which can embrace not only the natural and man-made catastrophes by which we are surrounded, but which, by a supreme act of collective courage, can face the possible destruction of our world. Walter de la Mare, writing about death, once compared the human race to children kept in a giant's kitchen and disappearing one by one. The survivors continued to play as if nothing had happened, ignoring the sudden departures of their playmates. The reality of death is with us always; we are more human if we can live in the light of it, better able to comfort one another. When part of that reality is suffering, or the destruction of things and places that are precious to us, there is more, not less, reason to grow up into the tragic vision. Like the aged Oedipus, we will find that suffering and self-knowledge go hand in hand.

Yet we shall need the corrective of the ironic vision if we are not to dramatise ourselves, or harbour grandiose ideas about our own 'specialness'. We shall need to be able to note the rich absurdities of life, the funny things that happen on the most solemn occasions, our ludicrous earnestness. If we are to be the victims of a tragedy, then that tragedy can, in turn, be viewed with detachment — we are lost amid a million human tragedies. It is no worse with us than with the others. If we can find a way through (and we are more likely to do it with the aid of the ironic vision than any of the others) we shall still need irony to help us with the private tragedy of our own death.

Are there any signs that we have yet begun to acquire a response to life which, while preserving 'the sense of religion' (meaning) of which Tebelak speaks yet passes beyond the comic and romantic vision, and includes an awareness of the tragic and ironic visions? There are as yet only sprouting seeds to be seen, some to be found where one might expect, in contemplative circles, both Christian and other, some in communities, some in psychoanalytic circles, some in the theatre and in other arts. There are signs of it in the Underground with its belief in a new warmth between people that is based not on sentiment, but a realistic assessment of how badly we need one another, signs of it in the pop songs which can show such wisdom about death, or sex, or human folly.

> There'll come a time when all of us must leave here
> Then nothing Sister Mary can do
> Will keep me here with you
> As nothing in this life that I've been trying
> Can equal or surpass the Art of Dying.

> There'll come a time when all your hopes are fading
> When things that seemed so very plain
> Become an awful pain
> Searching for the truth among the lying
> And answered when you've learned the
> Art of Dying.[8]

With the ecological problem constantly with us as a *memento mori*, with an awareness that we need to grow up and beyond our romantic one-sidedness into some better grasp of the tragic and ironic aspects of our life, how do we set about our journey now? Our lively apprehension of death, decay and destruction could push us towards pessimism and despair, or it could heighten our awareness of being alive, and our compassion to one another. Man has often found joy and meaning in conditions of great insecurity.

Obviously if we can avert catastrophe in the forms of starvation, pollution and war then we must try to do so, but if we cannot, either to the degree of total destruction, or to the lesser degree we have witnessed in such places as East Bengal, then our understanding will need to acquire dimensions that we can as yet scarcely guess at. We shall need to shed many national,

8 George Harrison, 'All Things Must Pass'.

political, and commercial prejudices which at present make any effective sharing of our resources almost impossible in order to relieve suffering that can be relieved. Yet we shall also need, on our own behalf and that of others, to learn something about living with suffering that cannot be relieved.

In addition we shall need all kinds of new approaches, some of which in themselves may relieve our problems to a degree we can as yet hardly know. This means a readiness to question everything, to go back over dearly held and hardly won beliefs and prejudices and examine them afresh, not from the 'common-sense' point of view alone (common-sense always tending to be egocentric and concerned with our own mental or physical safety) but also from the point of view of love of our fellow-men, particularly the fellow-men we don't much care for.

Whether we shall have the heart to do any of these things turns, in my view, on whether people can, in general, recapture a 'religious' approach to life. We have seen how, in the pop and Underground scenes, and even in some branches of the commercial theatre, there are signs of a feeling for 'religion', how certain trends, such as drug-taking indicate, even if rather pathetically, the need to discover a journey, and how certain aspects of 'conventional' religion, such as the Pentecostalists on the one hand, and the contemplative orders on the other, remind us that an old tree like the Church can still produce green shoots and blossom. Among orthodox Christian believers there is an acute suspicion of, and sometimes superiority towards, other religious approaches; the years roll back and for a moment one sees Christianity as it was in its origins, one cult trying desperately to differentiate itself from the myriad pagan cults that surrounded it. Or as it was later, a body of doctrine, trying to defend itself against heresies, some of which appear, even with hindsight, to be just as cranky and dangerous as they appeared to main stream Christians at the time.

Many human errors seem to result from rigidly applying lessons learned in history to situations where they no longer apply, and I have a feeling that the old back-to-the-wall response to paganism, or the old struggle to keep the doctrine pure and the cranks in their proper place (too often, the place of painful execution) is now an inappropriate and inauthentic response to the human situation. If, as seems likely, we are about to see every kind of religious interest, cranky or otherwise, flourish in our midst, then we have the choice either of holding rigidly to one particular form of belief, or of trying to hear what this babble of different voices is trying so urgently to tell us. It would be a pity if we tried to compare this situation to earlier situations, for instance that of ancient Rome, for though the religions may be markedly similar to those of earlier times, we who hear about them are very different people. We can see how often heresy consisted of what the main body of believers were intent on repressing (thus together with the main body of belief working towards a wholeness of meaning), and we must ask ourselves if we still need to maintain those earlier repressions and if so, why.

If religion is, as I would define it, a sense of journey or quest, then we shall be releasing men from bondage if we are prepared to admit that the journey takes many bizarre forms, not all of them recognisable as such to others. Christianity has often tried to insist that the journey must take a particular form, i.e. that there is no salvation outside the Church, and this defensive belief may have done incalculable damage to those who could not manage to make their journey take that form, but were too discouraged to seek elsewhere. Graham Greene's Scobie in *The Heart of the Matter* pitifully illustrates the destruction of a brave and profoundly religious man who simply could not manage to conform to the kind of journey required of him. English Catholicism in the Thirties was admittedly provincial to an exceptional degree, but it held in its net men of the highest intelligence, such as Waugh and Greene, who refused to see how life-denying their chosen belief had become. (Greene has, of course, exposed the deathliness of a sick Christianity in this novel, but he does not strike the final blow for freedom, which is to show that Scobie is ludicrous as well as tragic).

What makes Christians hesitate to encourage real freedom of belief in others, or to tread strange paths themselves, is a deep sense that Christianity is special, that it has unique characteristics which make it quite different from any of the other major religions and that if others will not accept this then they are in error. For some Christians this takes the form of wanting others to 'know' Christ, or to 'make a decision for him', for some it means recognising the centrality of the cross and the resurrection. And for some in both of these groups there is a spoken or tacit assumption that the aim of the Church is to persuade everyone else to agree with the Christians, and to join with them in a group expression of this truth, with or without ritual.

I want to suggest that this approach, which I call 'provincial' because it distorts the total picture of man with a 'local' view which ignores important facts, has confused the *kind* of truth which Christianity has to offer. Instead of saying, what I believe to be true, that every human journey faithfully made contains the experience of crucifixion and resurrection, and so partakes of the Christ-experience, the provincial approach insists that particular attitudes must be held to the death and resurrection of a historical personage and often to much else. The first approach allows creativity to the individual in giving him the chance to recognise something for himself; the second approach denies him creativity, insisting that he must experience in terms defined by others or his experience cannot possibly be authentic.

The Churches bear all too clearly at the present time the marks of non-creativity in their members, and it seems possible that the cut-and-dried nature of their attitudes attracts those for whom creativity is difficult. But journey is not about being 'cut-and-dried', but on the contrary about living, and living is altogether an untidy, unpredictable, trial-and-error kind of process. If the Churches come to represent death then it would be better that others should not come and join them, but that those inside them should go out into the world, try to find the places where there is life, and try to learn what those who have life are able to teach.

The error which I believe has allowed those of us who are Christians to fall into provincialism is the error of forgetting that religions are only a metaphor for what is beyond metaphor. Because Christianity is such a strikingly real and apt metaphor for the human experience of God, perhaps the best metaphor man has yet found, it is the more tempting to forget that it does not measure at all adequately to the shape and quality of the experience itself. And because we are afraid of the numinous we may insist all the more frantically that it may only present itself to us in forms that we already recognise and are used to. In many Christian circles there is a sort of 'thought-stop' at the point where it is suggested that the form a man's religion takes may not be of very great importance. What is still thought to be necessary is 'commitment', and commitment is seen in terms of

church-going, baptism, receiving Communion or whatever the
accepted form may be. These things are thought to be life-giving,
and those who do not do them are thought to be cut off from the
springs of life. But what if it is commitment, not to formal
Christianity, but to the numinous journey, which constitutes life?
In that case, some will be found within the Christian fold, some
in other folds, Buddhist, Jewish, Vedantic, Islamic, etc., and some
in no recognised fold at all.

The practising Christian would describe this as 'dangerous',
believing that errors would creep in if the journey were denied
the strength of Christian supervision. But the truth may be, as all
the mythical journeys make clear, that *all* journeys are dangerous,
that some error is unavoidable, even necessary, and that
important stretches of it must, in any case, be made in loneliness
in which no one but the traveller seems to know where he is
going. And when there are counsellors they do not necessarily
take the form of traditional piety; Circe, for example, is scarcely
the Christian ideal.

But if the traveller does not need to 'know' Christ, in the sense
in which Christians use this term, before starting on his journey,
I believe that it is impossible that he will not do so, in a far more
intimate sense, when he is fully engaged upon it. Christ as the
archetype of the journeying hero is an unavoidable discovery
for those who take the numinous journey, Malory's 'worshipful
way', at all seriously. He is known not as a historical person, but
as a dynamism within the individual's experience. There is no
need for him to be given the name of Christ, any more than there
is need for the individual to call himself a Christian. What is
needed is for him to recognise that he has reached the heart of the
human experience, and to long to be more of a human being
more than he longs for anything else in this life. It is for this that
he must renounce false strength, lies, and pretence about his own
omnipotence, and it is in hope of this that he must live and try
to love his brother.

Wanting only to be a more human human being, and recognising the need for brokenness and poverty of spirit to reach this
humanity, the traveller begins to acquire a very different attitude
to moral issues. What is gone is the 'lust for ideals', a lust which
Zen regards as quite as troublesome as the lusts of the flesh. The
'lust for ideals' leads to a one-sidedness, which gives an

unexpected power to evil. The man who suffers from it is as much in bondage as the man who is at the mercy of his desires.

Anyone who repudiates the lust for life because he is caught in the lust for ideals has not advanced in the most fundamental sense. True, he is further advanced than the unthinking man of desires, since he is conscious of both sides and understands the irreconcilable tension between them. But he has not yet gone far enough: he is not yet beyond the opposites, living out of a truth that has superseded them. Therefore, he meets with rejection. The priest who sees in this only malevolence, becomes all the more demanding, thinks himself superior, and is full of reproaches for the wicked and intolerant, not yet free from the desire for recognition, honour, even veneration. There is an unadmitted power-drive at work in him, and his 'cure of souls' is largely an expression of this is the guise of holy zeal and moral superiority[9]

Zen, like Christianity, thinks that the human journey is about achieving an 'ego-less' state. 'Ego-self, till now the secret or conscious point of reference for all everyday experiences, must vanish.' Perhaps no human being ever achieves this goal, except fleetingly; one of the most touching and thoroughly human things about the Zen stories is that even great spiritual masters are apt to do or say foolish or misguided things, in the intervals of sublime teaching, and need taking down a peg or two. And in the act of admitting their weakness and folly, they command more respect for the courage of their humanity than in their most inspired moments. It is not success that counts.

What does count is a quality of love that emerges as often from failure to be good, as from the exercise of virtue itself. It is a love which has a certain impartiality. 'This means rejoicing when something happens to me exactly as I would if it happened to someone else, and sorrowing under another's sorrow no less than if it befell me. . . . This love . . . does not woo, does not obtrude itself, make demands, disquieten, or persecute, which does not give in order to take, possesses an astounding power, precisely because it shuns all power.'[10]

[9] Eugen Herrigel, *Method of Zen* (Routledge & Kegan Paul, 1960).
[10] Ibid.

Clearly it is unlikely to lay down the law about what others should or should not do because it can enter into the motives and drives of others nearly as easily as into its own, and can also see its own motives with a shocking clarity which inhibits the condemnation of others.

Sexual morality is one of the main fields with which organised religion has concerned itself, understandably, since sex is, for most human beings, the 'quick' of feeling, the place where they are most thoroughly aware of being themselves.

Here, the 'lust for ideals' and the romanticism out of which it springs, has made for an inflexibility and an arbitrariness which has made us deny the spirit, and the knowledge that the 'wind bloweth where it listeth' in this area of our lives as in all others and is not to be bounded by expediency.

What this means in practice is that we shall have to recognise a very much wider range of 'legitimate' relationships if we are to allow people the freedom to make the journeys which beckon them. The old rules about pre-marital sex and adultery which were widely broken in practice need to be viewed as the roughest of guides, reminders that life is inextricably bound up with commitment, and that we cannot learn to live if, sooner or later, we do not recognise both the joy and the loss of being 'given'. Here again, as with the experience of Christ, we have made the mistake of taking what the wise and experienced discovered for themselves by trial-and-error, and binding it upon the foolish and the naive as something they *ought* to experience. But for many the ability to commit themselves wholly to a one-to-one relationship is only possible after innumerable other 'adventures', and for others the attempt to bind themselves at far too early a point in their journey means an impoverishment that leads to despair. They can never meet their Circe or Siduri or Beatrice, because they have been trained to believe that salvation cannot lie in that direction. Or if they succeed in discovering her, they are forced to conform to the convention that treats all extra-marital loves between men and women as squalid and exclusively carnal.

Even in what is described as a 'permissive' society, this attitude is still widely held. Television plays propagate the idea that for a wife to discover that there is 'another woman' in her husband's life is about the worst thing that can happen to her, and that she is bound to exhibit the most primitive signs of jealousy, rather than show the slightest concern about what spiritual or psychological importance this relationship might have for her partner. I cannot remember a single play which suggested that she might understand or even be glad for him, nor try to see the situation in any light besides a desperate peril to herself.

Our fear of a gentler attitude to one another's loves even pervades our myths about the famous. A series about C. G. Jung, put out by the B.B.C. at the time of writing, managed to leave out any reference to the women in his life, apart from his wife, who were important to his development. Its most serious distortion was to omit any reference to Antonia Wolff, who aroused the interest in Eastern thought which was to be one of the most important factors in his later development. Presumably the B.B.C. felt that this would detract from their determined presentation of Jung as a saintly old man; we have never quite recovered from the medieval feeling that saints ought to be celibate, or at the very least the husbands of elderly women.

This kind of hypocrisy has to go if, as individuals (or indeed corporately) we are to recover the sense of meaning in our lives, and help one another to embark upon the journeys which alone can save us from suicidal despair.

This is not, as its opponents seem to believe, a charter for sexual lust and the renunciation of all responsibility towards others. In fact, there are only two things which are able to keep our lust and our selfishness under control. One is fear, and the other is a strong sense of journey which gives unity to all our fallible attempts at relationship and inspires a compassion for those whom we meet on the way. We have tried fear in every possible form, fear of hellfire, fear of public disgrace, fear of disease, fear of pregnancy, fear of our partner; it has been quite astonishingly unsuccessful in containing the power of the sexual drive, and the longing for wholeness which underlies it. And it has led to an extraordinary callousness on the part of the conventionally religious, as they have refused to notice the cries for healing which could not be heard inside a particular marriage.

The trouble is that Christians are not very happy with the thought that the 'wind bloweth where it listeth' — they want it to blow where they tell it, and in the end it is this lack of trust or hope, this sense that things do work out if we let them and don't try to manipulate them, that is so destructive of relationship, and makes it impossible to talk honestly about sex in religious circles. People, it is felt, will do something terribly wicked if given half a chance. It is this form of heresy which is perhaps the greatest threat Christianity has ever encountered and which steadily undermines its basic truth.

But whatever conventional religion has to say about it, it is clear that a very different attitude to sexual relationships has come to stay, one that is not geared solely to marriage, but yet which rejects the 'naughtiness' with which extra-marital relationships have hitherto been regarded. This is partly a rejection of bourgeois hypocrisy, and 'safety first', but also is partly the sign of a new awareness of the importance of every kind of ecstatic experience in our lives. It is as if we have discovered that there is an inner ecological problem as well as an outer one. Overpopulation, urbanisation, commercial pressure, technology, have not only robbed us of precious qualities in our environment, but have made us aware that we have become spectators in life, not participating very much or very often in rewarding interchange with our neighbours. Without such interchange we cannot feel fully alive, and we have turned more gratefully and with deeper awareness to the kind of interchange that is still available to us. We refuse to regard it as trivial or as wicked, as our ancestors so blindly managed to do, and instead have chosen to reinstate it along with all that is most truly human. Sex, alongside mystical experience, and certain aesthetic experiences, is about unity, the opposite of the fragmentation with which we know ourselves to be so painfully threatened. It is also, of course, upsetting to the side of us which fears the loss of control, the selflessness, which all unifying experiences demand.

For the young this new attitude to sex is linked with a new sense of community in which people who try to be naturally themselves are not subjected to fierce critiques of their behaviour. Community is seen to be linked to a lack of fear of the body. Touching is no longer a threat, since physical closeness is no longer the thing which is only permitted under the most stringent conditions. It is possible for boys and girls, men and women, to forego the coyness and artificiality which have poisoned relations between the sexes for so long.

However, it is unlikely that even this freedom of approach will touch the real roots of our problem. A warmer community life, a lack of sexual inhibition, make it possible for people to admit the wounds which trouble them, but they may not by themselves bring about decisive changes which prevent us destroying others. If we listen to the inter-personal problems of any close-knit group, or even to the marital problems of any particular couple, we quickly begin to see how difficult it is to bring about any creative change. The story of each person concerned is complete, convincing, and in a sense, true, even when it directly contradicts the evidence of others; the real contradiction lies not in words or events, but in the way each interprets what happens according to their upbringing and pathology. It is this pattern, the pattern of upbringing and pathology, that we must get beyond in order to resolve the situations of deadlock — between marriage partners, parents and children, colleagues, parties, countries — which kill and destroy.

Churches have often talked as if they can help here, but in fact few religious people have the knowledge of psychological processes to solve such puzzles except by laborious trial-and-error. It is here, it seems to me, that psychoanalysis has everything to offer, if it can find ways of offering it in ordinary language. This is not a very rewarding task. There is hostility and ridicule of psychological insights, partly, one must assume, because of 'resistance', the unwillingness of those who have not undergone analysis to consider ideas which threaten their defensive systems. Dr. James Hillman, writing in *The Journal of Analytical Psychology* makes the point that psychoanalysis feels tainted to most people because it deals with the side of life they don't much care to think about, the side to do with weakness, defectiveness, absence of victory, bankruptcy, deception, lack and incompletion; in short with failure. Failure, like death, is a painful subject to dwell upon.

Yet without some willingness on the part of individuals and larger groups to look at their failures, however humiliating these may be, there can be no life-giving change. Each of us must remain locked in compulsive patterns, too near to our own problems even to know what they are until they are writ large upon the lives of those around us. It is easier to recognise the pathology of others than our own (as Jesus said a long time ago), but we may not therefore assume that we are healthier than they are.

Psychoanalysis appears to remind us of truths that conventional religion has pushed out of sight (though they are truths which appear in some other religions which are now becoming popular in this country). One of them is that we cannot be all goodness, nor can we lose the side of ourselves that is not good. To be whole people we need awareness of both our good and bad sides, and if we refuse to recognise our badness and deny it, then it becomes destructive as we project it outwards upon others and then start to persecute them. The madness which seizes men as they project this badness upon minority groups, or upon their opponents, as we have seen in Northern Ireland, is the most terrifyingly inhuman thing we are ever asked to witness. In such situations men cease to be recognisably human. Nor is it only in such extreme situations. In innumerable conversations in which each of us join with neighbours or colleagues or even with casual acquaintances upon a train, violent prejudices with the same total irrationality behind them appear; groups or individuals are condemned, without compassion, and we sense that it is not truth that is important, but some inner satisfaction of the speaker. We are all caught up in such delusive systems, and we each try to involve others in them. Fortunately we usually fail and no real communication takes place, but there are those whose delusive systems are so fascinating that others do accept their strange laws, becoming voluntarily mad. Trying *not* to be more deluded than we can help is an exhausting and unending struggle in which the trained mind of the analyst can be indispensable, though other factors, such as close personal relationships, can also be important.

Another important contribution of analysis lies in its recognition of the self-punishing nature of man. Where Christianity has often noticed the vanity and pride of man, analysis notices rather his self-loathing and his temptations towards self-destruction. Not that these things are in any way exclusive of one another; they can exist side by side in the same personality without difficulty — perhaps they are different faces of the same coin. Man's cruelty towards himself can lead him to deny himself the love without which he cannot live, and the conditions of living which enable him to make his journey. Analysis insists that we 'set up' the conditions in which we live, including much that we have chosen to regard as accidental misfortune, such as illness, poverty, unattractiveness or professional ups and downs. So that where life is intolerably painful either to individuals, or collectively it is that they may have unconsciously 'chosen' such a way to live, either to punish themselves, or because they guess that only by such a route can they lay hold of a particular truth or experience that they need. The second has everything to do with journey, the first very little, except to prevent it. But the act of preventing is worth studying, since we have a way of allowing ourselves everything, except the thing we long for most, which may, in fact, be our 'journey'.

When we see as much collective suffering and despair as we do at the present time, so many prophets of doom, and so few who talk eagerly and hopefully about the future, or even contentedly about the present, it seems worth considering how far we are being ridden by collective self-hatred. We may have jumped upon a nightmare that we do not want, and lack the courage, the naive courage, to jump off again, and start loving our humanity enough to want to save it.

How shall we save our humanity? First of all, I believe, by giving pride of place to ecstasy in all the forms in which we know it, placing wholeness first, the wholeness to which all journeys are laboriously working, and of which we have all had intimations in rare ecstatic moments. When our sense of the meaningfulness of our lives is so precarious then primacy must be given to ecstasy as to all rare and irreplaceable resources. I do not mean that we must seek to conjure ecstatic experience, though we could afford to be far less condemnatory to those who feel the need to do so through such methods as 'trips', but rather that we must try to understand and seek to perpetuate the situations in which ecstasy, and near-ecstasy, can be naturally come by.

Man has always had his methods — loneliness and silence, various forms of sensory deprivation, prayer, art, sexual intercourse, group experiences, particularly those involving singing and dancing, drug-taking in the form of eating particular plants or drinking particular liquids. Primitive peoples quite naturally and unselfconsciously incorporate ecstatic forms of experience in their lives, unconsciously aware that they need such *foci* if they are to have the power to continue. For them the threat is loss of fertility either in their crops, their animals, or themselves. For us the danger is a loss of creativity, and we have the task of trying to achieve consciously what they achieve unconsciously.

We need to treasure all these forms of achieving ecstasy as

the most precious possessions we have, and to recognise that while some people are gifted or daring in experiencing a number of them, everyone needs to experience in at least one of these modes if their lives are to retain any point and purpose. Great charity is needed in this, as in all areas of our lives, in recognising that what is important to us may not be important to others, and equally, that what is important to others may not speak at all to us; whatever happens we must not trample upon one another's green shoots, since it is here that life is and it is painfully easy to murder one another's timorous attempts at growth.

It is interesting to notice that while some forms of ecstasy seem to depend upon the attempt to set the senses on one side, others depend upon using the senses unreservedly, almost to the point where they fuse in a non-sensory reality. I should perhaps explain that I regard the many states of mind which border upon ecstasy, as almost as important as the state itself. There are many, many frames of mind — to do with the sudden perception of people or of objects, with moments of joy or of grief, with feelings of being 'there', with feelings of love, with experiences of time or space dissolving, with the satisfaction of aesthetic feelings, and many more — which touch upon the ecstatic experience in ways that are deeply satisfactory without reaching the momentary loss of the ego which is the supreme experience. For many this ultimate loss feels too dangerous, too like madness, to be attainable, yet they may still get their nourishment from the border-lands of ecstasy, and perhaps occasionally from the few who can tolerate ecstasy. Perhaps our human task is to learn gradually to allow a little more and a little more ecstasy into our lives, on each occasion holding the door open a little longer before slamming it shut on what is overwhelming.

Many, perhaps most, human beings can remember having ecstatic experiences in early childhood, and some have a powerful recurrence in adolescence or in early adulthood. But then, perhaps because of the need for energetic adaptation to the world around us, in terms of finding jobs, bearing and raising a family — the tasks with which the majority of people fill their twenties and thirties — this special kind of awareness seems to disappear. But it can recur in middle age, and even perhaps reach a kind of flowering in old age. Writing, from a Christian standpoint, in

Theoria to Theory Julia de Beausobre suggests that something rather similar is the vocation of old age, where what she calls 'fruitful leisure in solitude' is permitted the old.

By the time we have become noticeably less alert, the bulk of our general understanding increases and deepens remarkably, as if a different part of the brain — a fresh or well rested part — were taking over from an outworn part which for years has been selecting with incalculable speed the particular sense which at any moment has to be given immediate priority over every other activity. The shift in predominance from alertness to overall understanding in depth creeps in unnoticed if our mental energy does not begin to flag before the body is sufficiently outworn to begin tangibly to expire.[11]

Where the old are able to reach this different kind of concentration, then, according to Julia de Beausobre, 'concepts acquire a new creative quality. They move out of linear formation and freed of logical linkages, regroup into clusters or patterns that can be called harmonies. To live in a harmony of concepts is unlike stopping to enjoy for a while a harmony of emotions. No emotion belongs to the sphere of tranquillity; but harmonies of concepts are part of it, and they are fuel for the fire called divine love.' To achieve this new awareness she feels that 'worn out people need much leisure free of external stress', but the cost of providing this, to the young and the robust middle-aged, can be seen as being repaid by the special quality of awareness that the old can become qualified to provide for the whole community.

This special awareness which the old can achieve in the right conditions has, I believe, other modes which are appropriate to different ages and temperaments. What seems inimical to it in all circumstances is fierce activity, together with the tension, the competitiveness, the self-importance, and the very superficial awareness of others which this engenders. Compulsions of all kinds work against contemplative awareness, since they make any 'letting go' impossible. In so far as our way of life is determinedly 'busy', and we continue to applaud those who work too hard and exhort our children towards competitive attitudes, then we are hostile to ecstasy, the irruption of which is no respecter of

[11] Julia de Beausobre, *Theoria to Theory*, Vol. 5, October 1971.

our plans and ambitions and addictions, and which painfully reminds us what it is to be alive.

To live for ecstasy is to live very simply, making few claims upon life, though those few are enormous ones.

Thomas Merton, the Cistercian, has explored one particular way of achieving the awareness I am talking about, that of the hermit, who reaches the state through silence and solitude. For Merton, the hermit of the twentieth century has a very special contribution to make. Unlike earlier generations of hermits who showed that the grace of God could lead them into superhuman feats of strength and endurance, the twentieth-century hermit has the task of reminding men how to be simply human at a period when this is anything but easy for most people.

Whereas in the fourth century monks were determined to prove their solitude charismatic by showing it to be beyond the human, the situation today is quite the reverse. The whole of man's life is now pushed to extremes pressing him almost to his biological and psychological limit. Hence the mission of the solitary is first the full recovery of man's human and natural measure.[12]

A man who gets up at sunrise, and goes to bed when it is dark, who combines manual with intellectual labour, who lives close to nature, who is not continually manipulating himself out of boredom with television or radio or a busy social and professional life, is certainly leading a life very different from the rest of us. To what end? This man's first duty, says Merton, is 'to live happily and without affectation in his solitude'. This is more difficult than it sounds since, robbed of distraction, the hermit may become aware of psychological problems that the rest of us try not to notice in ourselves. Above all, according to Merton, he will have problems about his own identity, since solitude denies the continual assertion of ourselves that most people get from social intercourse. In his solitude he will undergo crises of a most painful kind, and he will discover as each of us must, that the idolatry of the self is the most difficult to overthrow, though also the most rewarding. But in time he learns that 'renouncing care and

[12] Thomas Merton, *Christian Solitude: Contemplation in a World of Action* (Allen & Unwin, 1971), p. 241.

concern about getting somewhere and having fun, he finds that to
live is to be happy, once one knows what it is to *live* in simplicity.'

This is not a specifically Christian insight, though there are
many features of Merton's thought which are. Similar thoughts
are to be found in Zen, which had an influence on Merton, as
well as among people who have no clearly defined religion. An
old German naturalist in Conrad's *Lord Jim* describes his understanding of the human lot like this: 'A man that is born falls into
a dream like a man who falls into the sea. If he tries to climb out
into the air as experienced people endeavour to do, he drowns. . . .
I tell you, the way is to the destructive element submit yourself,
and with the exertions of your hands and feet in the water make
the deep, deep sea keep you up.' He regards this patient swimming as a kind of humble and obedient following of one's destiny,
as day after day one finds the courage to submit oneself to the
'destructive element'. The way to be is to 'follow the dream, and
again to follow the dream — *usque ad finem*. . . .'

This kind of acceptance of what comes also has something of
The *I-Ching*'s sense of the ebb and flow of good fortune. Things
that we had not even hoped for are given freely to us, and things
that seemed our natural right are taken from us. 'You don't always
get what you want, but you sometimes get what you need.'

Of course, most of us are not going to live as hermits, and
for the biggest part of our lives we are not free to taste the particular freedoms of old age. Whatever ecstasy we know must
necessarily be worked out within a context of work and family
life, and if we prize our ordinary humanness beyond anything
else we possess, then we can be glad that we can take our journey
in this form, and not in any way that men tend to regard as somehow 'special'.

This kind of journey is a difficult one, since the leisure in
which to reach the awareness we need is so hard to come by, and
often seems only possible to achieve at the expense of others. If
we are going to fight for some relief from the insistent pressures
of our lives, then we need to feel sure that it is in some sense
for others, and not a selfish indulgence. *Not* to work always to
the point of exhaustion, or to the state of mind in which work
becomes an addiction, is, to begin with, an example. Others who
are driven by guilt can mark this act of moderation and take
bearings by it. Those who are worn out by work become in-

capable of any but the most superficial exchanges with their relatives, friends and colleagues, and to this extent are less human. They become inattentive to the beauties of the world around, locked in anxiety and fatigue which forbid any real perception. All values become distorted, as the capacity for play is lost. Life is so real, so earnest, that it becomes unrecognisable as itself; it is rather a kind of death.

Above all they become incapable of the sort of simple happiness which Merton describes, and begin to doubt, and to cause others to doubt, whether such happiness is even possible. Perhaps one of the things which ails our society is the exhaustion which comes from years of over-activity, so that we have forgotten about happiness and how to achieve it.

Some people can and do, however, achieve the sort of contemplative awareness I am speaking of within the context of 'ordinary' life. For some it comes at least partly through people; by making use of some particular capacity for loving others, friends, relatives, lovers, they point to a release from ceaseless activity. Love at once shows busyness up for the substitute and the escape that it is.

Or they may get more from a kind of solitude within a life crowded with people. Prayer, aesthetic experience are important to this kind of journey.

The young of our own time seem to find particular meaning in the group experience, though, like sexual experience, this can be intensely, vitally, meaningful to people of most age-groups.

Any of these journeys tend gradually to lessen the appetite for commercial gain, status and the expensive toys that go with it, since they show human life in a different perspective which makes such things look ridiculous. Drugs such as LSD also bestow this perspective, sometimes so suddenly and strongly that it becomes temporarily impossible to carry on the usual kind of life.

Such journeys, although they have their own kind of suffering, can also relieve kinds of personal suffering which otherwise plague us persistently. The bitterness of feeling that we have not achieved the degree of worldly success that we would have liked, and perhaps deserved, the pain of seeing our bodies grow old, the wound of sexual frustration, are all caught up and used within the context of the journey until our suffering is transformed.

Though every journey is individually determined, certain needs and experiences are common to all journeys. The experience of silence and of solitude is the ground of every journey, and within the silence the readiness to live out the depression which is the inescapable road to joy. Then, there must be some attempt at 'letting go', at enduring the inner emptiness and sense of falling, in order to discover our own liberating unimportance. Paradoxically, the attempt to lose the self leads to a new awareness both of ourself and others. In our rushed and anxious lives we train ourselves to ignore our own feelings, and to lose touch with the whole delicate range of sensibilities with which we are endowed. In a dialogue between Devi and Shiva on the subject of 'centreing' an Indian writer tries to speak of this experience of becoming aware of one's body: 'Feel: My thought, I-ness, internal organs — me.[13] Not out of the self-fascination which afflicts most of us, but as part of an exercise which sets the self free and transforms it. 'Feel the consciousness of each person as your own consciousness. So, leaving aside concern for self, become each being.' A certain lightness and detachment is needed in looking at the goings-on of the world around one, including one's own goings-on. 'This so-called universe appears as a juggling, a picture show. To be happy look upon it so.'[14]

Journey requires these meditative and contemplative moments in order that the traveller can work out where he is going and come to terms with the mistakes he has made. It is what men used to call prayer, but there is no need to limit it by the rather conventional and stereotyped ideas we have about prayer. If our lives are so arranged that there is enough opportunity for reflection, which means refusing to escape into the addiction of work (or other forms of addiction which blunt our awareness), then we shall not be able to escape the fear and longing to lose the self which is the crucial struggle of every journey. The journey, let me be clear, is not about becoming a saint or holy man (an incidental matter with which it is better not to concern ourselves) but about trying to become a human being.

This does not only come to us through solitude, of course, but wherever we are engaged, happily or otherwise, in relationship with others. Love is both the most cruel and the most heal-

[13] Paul Apps, *Zen Flesh, Zen Bones: A Collection of Zen and Pre-Zen Writings* (Penguin, 1971).
[14] Ibid.

ing of all instruments in tearing away the illusions and the projections by which we try to ease our pain. It summons us back continually from the comfortable madness in which we are 'somebody' into the painful sanity in which we know we are nothing. Yet in that nothing it shows us a peace and a joy and a dignity that is beyond anything we could have guessed at. It is a process identical with what Christians call 'repentance' — a continual rediscovery of one's weakness and dependence, which releases one from the burden of self-inflation. If one sees oneself as part of the 'picture show' as Devi recommends, then what one is watching is often very like high farce.

In the West we have tended to treat ourselves rather more seriously than this, carrying heavy burdens of guilt at our inability to resolve the dilemma of the self, and taking the darker aspects of our lives with a dramatic seriousness which has made detachment difficult. We have valued the individual human being at the expense of the natural world around him, taking him, as it were, out of context, rather than seeing him woven into a larger pattern in which tragedy — the tragedy of disease, flood, earthquake, avalanche, famine — plays a part. Our insistence on the goodness of God — by which we mean goodness as we, with all our limitations, are able to measure it — has made us particularly unwilling to believe that any form of human suffering could be contained within the will of God.

Perhaps the way through all the suffering which lies ahead of us will be to combine some of the Eastern detachment with the Western concern — to care for the individual body and its suffering as meticulously as we can (because feeling is important — an awareness that we must not try to deaden) — while recognising that in an eternal context it doesn't matter at all, whether the suffering is our own or other people's. I do not wish to suggest that the tragedy of suffering is not felt as absolute at the time, and this is why it demands vigorous efforts to overcome it; only that time is not the whole truth about man and his suffering. The glory of Christianity has been that, perhaps alone among religions, it has concerned itself with the tragedy of man *within time*, and so given its attention to suffering and failure. Crucifixion and resurrection, rightly understood, are sublime insights achieved into what the nature of humanity is, and what its relation is to divinity. And yet the less dramatic insights about detachment, and the 'picture show' that is the world are also of crucial importance, and our inability to grasp them itself produces untold suffering, particularly perhaps at the level of 'power struggles' and inter-personal conflict. In our desperation for 'life' we are apt to strew death and destruction all about us.

> The people treat death lightly:
> It is because the people set too much store by life
> That they treat death lightly.[15]

Side by side with the question of suffering, we must consider the question of individual sacrifice. Here the conflict is not so much between Christianity and other forms of religion, as between ancient and modern understanding of spirituality. Many Christians, like many of other faiths, have considered the extinction of desire, together with the forms of asceticism which lead up to it, as central to their journey. If we have begun to have doubts about it, it is because we have seen how easily it can be used as an escape route from the fullness and wholeness to which journey should lead a man. It is easy to despise the body because we cannot bear to be bound to it and its weaknesses; if we lose it by repression then we can kid ourselves that we are stronger than we are. Or we may avoid desire because of our fear of the ecstasy which is its goal; we sense that through it we may be called to more costly forms of journey which we fear. Or we may hate ourselves so profoundly that we feel obliged to deny ourselves the things which bring the greatest joy. All of these possibilities have made the old idea of the extinction of desire suspect, and yet like most ancient insights it speaks to us with a truth we cannot quite deny. It sometimes happens that when we are obliged to deny our desires we find ourselves emerging into a state of peace and joy which we might otherwise not have guessed at, and momentarily at least, we know that human happiness does not consist in total gratification, even if that were socially possible.

Nevertheless, to be fully human we need to know about desire and the gratification of desire, and we must not strive to be angels who miss this kind of longing and fulfilment. Perhaps the trouble

[15] Lao Tzu, *Tao te Ching*, tr. D. C. Lau (Penguin, 1969).

is that, as so often in Christian history, we have taken what
happens, almost of its own accord, to people who are far advanced
along their spiritual path, and recommended it to those who have
scarcely started. Desire, as normally understood, may get consumed in a still greater desire, the desire for God, yet this cannot
happen as an act of human will, but is rather a gift which comes
to those who have travelled courageously over rather earthier
territory.

I talk of the desire for God, but I am far from sure that all
human beings would wish to describe the aim of their journeys in
any kind of personal terms, though I think all would recognise
the truth of other journeys which did. Truth is so contradictory,
so paradoxical, so simple, and so unexpected, that there is room
for many varieties of experience. For some truth is God in a
personal sense, for others it is pantheist experience of the world,
and for others again it is a belief about wholeness. It is a pity if we
try to make others use our particular jargon, or if we even try to
pretend that their truth is identical with ours. And not only a
pity, but also an absurdity, since none of the jargon expressions
are in the least adequate to describe what we experience, and
that which is beyond metaphor eludes all our attempts to cap-
ture it.

Within the God-tradition this difficulty has been recognised
among those who follow what is known as the 'apophatic' way. In
this way men despair of knowing God by his presence (since his
presence is beyond anything that the human senses can hope to
comprehend) but seek instead to know him by his absence. It is
this absence of God, of the wholeness for which we long, that
journey is all about, since it is what journey seeks to rectify.

And if we arrive at journey's end? It is hard to know how many
do, since we cannot judge the achievement of others, but sometimes, in either the peace or the conflict of others we recognise
qualities which tell us how far they have got, and we are overwhelmed with respect. A few seem able to go beyond this, like
the aged Oedipus, but the rest of us must go as far as we can,
growing in the awareness which brings life to ourselves and
others.

The particular thing to learn is how to get to the crack between
the worlds and how to enter the other world. There is a crack

between the two worlds, the world of the *diableros* and the world of living men. There is a place where the two worlds overlap. The crack is there. It opens and closes like a door in the wind. To get there a man must exercise his will. He must, I should say, develop an indomitable desire for it, a single-minded dedication. But he must do it without the help of any power or any man. The man by himself must ponder and wish up to a moment in which his body is ready to undergo the journey. The moment is announced by prolonged shaking of the limbs and violent vomiting. The man usually cannot sleep or eat, and wanes away. When the convulsions do not stop the man is ready to go, and the crack between the worlds appears right in front of his eyes, like a monumental door, a crack that goes up and down. When the crack opens the man has to slide through it. It is hard to see on the other side of the boundary. It is windy, like a sandstorm. The wind whirls around. The man then must walk in any direction. It will be a short or a long journey, depending on his willpower. A strong-willed man journeys shortly. An undecided, weak man journeys long and precariously. After this journey the man arrives at a sort of plateau. It is possible to distinguish some of its features clearly. It is a plane above the ground. It is possible to recognise it by the wind, which there becomes even more violent, whipping, roaring all around. On top of that plateau is the entrance to that other world. And there stands a skin that separates the two worlds; dead men go through it without a noise, but we have to break it with an outcry. The wind gathers strength, the same unruly wind that blows on the plateau. When the wind has gathered enough force, the man has to yell and the wind will push him through. Here his will has to be inflexible, too, so that he can fight the wind. All he needs is a gentle shove; he does not need to be blown to the ends of the other world. . . .[16]

[16] Carlos Castenada, *The Teachings of Don Juan: Yaqui Way of Knowledge* (Penguin).